The *Vision* of MELVILLE *and* CONRAD

 *A COMPARATIVE STUDY*

by Leon F. Seltzer

OHIO UNIVERSITY PRESS : ATHENS

The Vision of MELVILLE *and* CONRAD

for JAN

ACKNOWLEDGMENTS

For their helpful comments on the original manuscript, I would like to thank George Hochfield, Leslie Fiedler, Leo Gurko, and Martin Pops. For expert editorial advice I would like also to thank Dennis Jacobs.

The last section of the Introduction appeared in somewhat different form in *Conradiana* (Summer 1969) and is reprinted with the permission of the editor.

FOREWORD

Since differences between the fiction of Melville and Conrad receive little attention here, let it be admitted at the start that the two authors had their own preoccupations. Melville, for example, returns again and again in his writing (though often surreptitiously) to the sad enigma of Deity and the practical failures of Christianity. Conrad, a most morally dedicated artist, repeatedly addresses himself to the values of honor, restraint, work, and tradition; and attempts to illustrate the shortcomings of various social and political systems. Technically, Melville is more concerned with the uses of allegory and parody, Conrad with such narrative devices as the shift in time and perspective. If these and other distinctions are left undeveloped, it is because this study's primary contention is that Melville and Conrad, as artists, responded to human experience in essentially the same way. Discrepancies between them in style and subject, it is felt, reflect more than anything else divergences in taste and temperament. If the present investigation were an "appreciation" of the two authors, it would surely have been obliged to attend to these matters of contrast. But since its interests center upon basic similarities of vision, upon broad parallels in philosophical and moral outlook as they are manifested in common literary themes and techniques, it hardly seems necessary—or even relevant—to elaborate upon artistic singularities. Put another way, this undertaking is not concerned with what makes Melville Melville or Conrad Conrad but with all that meaningfully relates the two writers. To elaborate upon their differences would only be to repeat once again what has been said about them many times individually. It would, further, be to violate the unity of this study and to undermine, gratuitously I think, the integrity of its thesis.

New York   L.F.S.

ix

CONTENTS

IV: THE TECHNIQUES OF INSCRUTABILITY

V: THE DILEMMA OF "HOW TO BE" AND THE LEAP TO VALUES

VI: MELVILLE AND CONRAD'S MODERNITY

INTRODUCTION

The nature of this investigation would seem today sufficiently familiar to require no special preliminary explanation. "Comparative studies"—partly because of the endless ingenuity of today's practicing critic and partly because of the currently exhausted state of contextualism—appear to be coming more and more into vogue. All the same, the approach taken here is essentially dissimilar from the bulk of such studies, and it may be of some use to outline in brief what it endeavors to accomplish and what it does not.

It does not, first of all, aim to study influence or to add another note to the encyclopedic chronicles of the world's literary history. Although Conrad did not publish his first book till four years after Melville's death, and although he had actually read (or read into) at least three of his fellow sea writer's books, including *Moby-Dick*, there is little reason to believe that any of his themes or techniques can legitimately be traced back to Melville. This is so not simply because he responded negatively to the Melville he knew—he was also repelled by the works of Dostoevsky, yet, as is easily demonstrated, substantially influenced by them. It is, rather, that Conrad's affinities with Melville are such that while we might without exaggeration speak of them as "kindred spirits," it would be foolish to speak of Conrad's having schooled himself on Melville. For there is very little that Conrad could have learned from his limited sampling of the American author. The exoticist of *Typee* and *Omoo* could have nothing instructive to offer such a self-conscious artist as Conrad, and the rhapsodist of *Moby-Dick* — with all that book's cetological digressions, artificial heightenings of language, and devious narrative turns — could not but leave the level-headed author of "Heart of Darkness" cold and critical. It may seem a bit unjustified, then, to assert that the whole point of this study is that the creative impulses of Melville and Conrad are definable in very much the same terms, that their fictional worlds are, in both form and substance, revelatory of an extremely similar world view. Nevertheless, the level at which the two writers bear most comparison is so deeply fundamental, so intimately connected with their vision of man and the universe, that any influences by Melville on Conrad that we might predicate would probably seem superficial by comparison. Granted, owing to certain diversities in background and temperament, the artistic appeals of Melville and Conrad differ — sufficiently so that outside of the basic circumstance that both employed the sea as a symbolic backdrop for their dramas, critics have drawn few meaningful connections between them. A close look at their most important fiction, however, supplemented by an occasional reference to their letters, essays, and some of their minor novels and stories, should explain how a strikingly similar outlook on life led, in the process of artistic creation, to the adoption of common themes and techniques.

The results to be achieved through such an approach can, I think, be far more valuable and stimulating than those gained from studies designed principally to suggest what an author learned from some immediate predecessor. We might, for example, consider the recent scholarship that has sought to call attention to Cooper's influence on Melville. Focusing on *The Red Rover* and *The Sea Lions*, these critics have pointed out correspondences between them and Melville's sea tales (particularly *Moby-Dick*) with regard to character and event, authenticity of detail, romanticism of texture coupled with realism of tone, and the discernible attempt in both authors to make of the maritime adventure a serious, adult subject.[1] Most important, perhaps, is Thomas Philbrick's remark that "without *The Sea Lions* and its predecessors Melville's great novel could hardly have come into being."[2] But this observation, however valid, pertains to the *form* of *Moby-Dick,* not to its philosophical "divings"; thus, although it may tell us something important about Melville's literary frame of reference when he approached his epic work, it suggests little about the profound forces that gave that work its unique shape. More telling, then, in the study of Melville's creative imagination would be the comment by Perry Miller that "Melville, unlike Cooper, employed the pattern of the romance to explode the romantic thesis."[3] In short, Cooper's influence on Melville is not such as to lend itself to a detailed comparative study of the two authors, because the *spirit* of Melville, the informing vision of almost all his undertakings, is essentially different from Cooper's. At this more abstract perceptual level, one must look to Hawthorne or Shakespeare on matters of influence, not to the sea novels of a near contemporary.

Turning briefly to Conrad, we might enumerate various stylistic resemblances between his work and that of Flaubert. But here, too, although the examination of the introverted artistry of the French writer might enable us to define more exactly the nature of Conrad's controlling aesthetic, it would be almost useless in yielding conclusions about his moral and metaphysical positions as they emerge creatively. Moving from France to England, and to the sprawling productions of the Victorian novelists, we naturally expect to find much less basis for comparison. But even here we might note the affinities Conrad shared with the ever-influential Dickens—noting at the same time that such connections do not offer us much assistance in determining anew "the essential

[1]See A.R. Humphreys, *Herman Melville* (New York, 1962), p. 65; Perry Miller, "Melville and Transcendentalism," *Virginia Quarterly,* XXIX (1953), 568; Thomas Philbrick, *James Fenimore Cooper and the Development of American Sea Fiction* (Cambridge, Mass., 1961), pp. 264-265.

[2]P. 265.

[3]P. 557.

Conrad." The way the author's grubby London in *The Secret Agent* and *Chance* harks back to Dickens' handling of it, as well as many interesting similarities in character conception (revolving around the comic, the morbid, and the grotesque), have already been treated convincingly in print.[4] But despite the validity of such a linking, we are still forced to acknowledge that Dickens' *thesis* is hardly identifiable with Conrad's.

The present approach, though philosophical to an extent, has nothing to do with matters of *Zeitgeist*. Indeed, with Melville and Conrad representing two fairly distinct cultural eras, it could not justifiably handle such concerns anyway. And besides the half-century that separates Conrad's most important fiction from Melville's, there is the crucial fact that both writers lie outside the intellectual mainstream of their times. Finally, it should be brought out that this study is not concerned with any transcendent mythic or archetypal patterns in the fiction of the two authors; nor is it interested in examining their works in the light of modern depth psychology. Along such lines, definite correspondences could be (and have been) shown, but far from providing a solid foundation for examining their fiction, such relationships have the unfortunate effect of breaking down the works under consideration into mere examples of timeless psychic or ritualistic structures. At once the approach enlarges upon the literature it treats and reduces its artistic fullness so that it may the better "submit" itself to the generalities of social science.

All this is by way of qualification: to indicate what this study does not intend to deal with and to give some explanation why. To begin a more positive statement of purpose, however, by saying that it wishes to illustrate through concrete example how the works of one author may be used as a commentary, or critique, on those of another, would hardly be to say anything new. Several critics have by now suggested this valuable function of the comparative approach. But even though this notion has found general accept-

[4]Frederick R. Karl, "Conrad's Debt to Dickens," *Notes and Queries*, IV (1957), 398-400.

ance, very little has been done with it aside from the popular ana-
logical device of mentioning, by the way, one writer who may
conveniently "shed light upon" another—the latter being usually
the author in question, who is the only real subject of the comparison and who alone stands to profit from it. Although critics have
very frequently linked Melville and Conrad in passing, the relationship drawn between them has rarely done more than define some
aspect of one more vividly. Nor, in all fairness, was such a comparison meant to do more, since we may safely assume that the critic
making it never really considered the possibility of its having profound implications about the deepest creative impulses of both
writers. On the other hand, there have been critics who have
coupled Melville and Conrad by way of contrast. But here the
conclusions, while accentuating certain differences that exist between the two writers, have the unhappy result of obscuring a
more essential relationship between them, and thus concealing as
much as they reveal. To enumerate and evaluate all the random
examples of "footnote criticism" on the two authors would neces-
sitate a lengthy chapter in itself. And so the largely thankless task
is avoided here, especially since it would be largely pedantic—
devoted mostly to finding fault with, or refuting altogether, comments that were never meant as a basis for a critical position in
the first place.[5]

[5]As Jessie Green, the author of the only recent article on the two authors,
has observed: "Obvious kinship has long made allusion to Conrad as common
a trope in Melville criticism as allusion to Melville in Conrad criticism"
("Diabolism, Pessimism, and Democracy: Notes on Melville and Conrad,"
Modern Fiction Studies, VIII [1962], 287).

Since Green's 19-page essay stands alone among contemporary criticism
in dealing with the two writers in other than a fleeting "cross-reference" fashion,
some brief note on the nature of its contents seems in order. Let it at once be
said that the article's title is all too descriptive of the miscellany of its concerns.
Not having, it would seem, finally resolved to himself the precise aim of his
inquiry, Green is led to employ a comparison-contrast technique which ultimately makes of his overall effort something less than the sum of its parts. Its
worthwhile topics of discussion include (1) Melville's and Conrad's handling of
the Negro and the symbolic meaning of blackness in their works generally,
(2) the two writers' relationship to the pessimistic thought of Schopenhauer,

As early as 1922, the critic Henry Canby, in an essay relating
Melville and Conrad, reflected: "It may be that others have set
'Moby Dick' beside the works of Conrad. Some one must have done
it, so illuminating in both directions is the result."[6] (But no doubt
critical distance from the two writers was not then such as to enable
one to establish many meaningful nonmaritime parallels between
them, and many of Canby's own attempts must strike us as curiously inept. Identifying Melville too closely with his protagonist Ahab,
and ignoring the metaphysical implications of a novel structured
as is *Moby-Dick,* he erroneously labels the American writer a
"transcendental philosopher." Moreover, by failing to consider any
works by Melville other than *Moby-Dick,* he is led to contrast the
two authors in a most deceptive manner. "Melville is a moral
philosopher," he writes, "Conrad a speculative psychologist."[7])
To give just one more example of the long-held critical notion that
Melville and Conrad are fit subjects for comparison, we might mention John Freeman's pioneering book on Melville (1926). After
remarking rather astutely on some resemblances in subject and
form between "Benito Cereno" and the works of Conrad, Freeman
is moved to speculate that these similarities would appear to mirror
"some spiritual likeness between the American novelist and the
Polish novelist, which others may more fully trace."[8]

This is, needless to say, the whole purpose of the present under-

---

and (3) their notions about primitivism. Yet Green's findings — interesting and
usually valid — are lacking in suggestiveness. Perhaps this is the reason why
his paper has failed, at least up to the present time, to inspire any further
Melville-Conrad studies in the academic periodicals.

One other critical work may be mentioned here: this is James Guetti's
The Limits of Metaphor: A Study of Melville, Conrad, and Faulkner (Ithaca,
New York: Cornell Univ. Press, 1967). Since the interests of this book, however, are theoretical and technical, and since it treats its three centers of attention separately (as individual manifestations of certain modern problems of
narrative structure), it is not, finally, of major importance in a comparative
investigation of Melville and Conrad.

[6]"Conrad and Melville," in his *Definitions: Essays in Contemporary
Criticism* (New York, 1922), p. 262.

[7]Pp. 264, 266.

[8]*Herman Melville* (New York, 1926), p. 149.

taking, and the skeletal synopsis of what little has been done on the topic should indicate its relative independence. It should be emphasized at the outset, therefore, that while much of the criticism published on Melville and Conrad separately has been taken into account, direct use has been made of only a fraction, which has been referred to much less for its specific content than for its suggestiveness with regard to this study's comparative outlook. The breadth of the affinities shared by Melville and Conrad is, in fact, suggested by the frequency with which critical statements on one have special pertinence to the other. A great number of technical and thematic descriptions of Melville's fiction can be transferred entire to Conrad's with equal accuracy, and vice versa.

But to speak of "theme" and "technique" as though they were autonomous entities in the fiction of the two writers is to obscure the fact that in art content determines form, just as form serves to define content. By systematizing resemblances between Melville and Conrad with this fundamental aesthetic principle in mind, we may demonstrate the likenesses in their creative vision organically. Further, by using Conrad's works as a commentary on Melville's (or the reverse), we may be able to say something of significance about literary creativity. Without simplifying the works in question, we may yet reach some conclusions about the relationship of different themes and techniques.

For a fairly obvious example of such correspondences, we might look at the impressionistic devices adopted by Melville and Conrad in "Benito Cereno" and *Lord Jim.* It can be shown that the use of more than a single narrative perspective is a technical outcome of the two writers' conviction that inward reality is never perceptible to any one observer and that the omniscient point of view must therefore be abandoned as life-betraying. Related to this idea is the felt necessity in both authors for abstract or figurative language. Aware of the inability of a naturalistic viewpoint to penetrate surfaces, they are impelled to get at the truth through convolutions of rhetoric, a tactic that serves to expand the point of view for communication of an essentially different kind. Such a situation very likely accounts for the frequency with which critics speak of the "voice" of the two writers. Rhetoric (like the multiple perspective) also may be seen as the technical correspondent to the theme of inscrutability, since it often "dramatizes" the two authors' ambivalent attitude toward their subjects. Lastly, these impressionistic devices may be understood as bringing about the openness of form characteristic of works such as "Benito Cereno" and *Lord Jim* and indicative of the tentative stance Melville and Conrad maintain toward their materials. Never having been fully apprehended, these materials can never be resolved and so are destined to remain teasingly ambiguous.

It should be stressed that since many writers may share thematic concerns without being closely related, anyone who seeks to investigate similarities among them must take care to ascertain whether the thematic affinities he has discovered actually reveal meaningful correspondences in vision. And what is probably the most crucial test in verifying the significance of one's equations is examining the techniques employed to "inform" the common themes. For only through such scrutiny can one reach any assurance that two authors had the same *idea* about their themes — which by themselves may be common property. As Milton Stern, writing on the currency of Melville's pervading themes, has pointed out: "quest, innocence, self and society, guilt, freedom, fate, and isolation were common, conscious preoccupations of his literary age."[9] Such an observation should be sobering to anyone tempted to definitive conclusions on two authors because of abundant thematic parallels noted between them. Unless there are substantial stylistic affinities as well, the resemblances so eagerly pounced upon may be of little significance. It may be recalled — as a spectacular sort of example — that two and a half centuries did not prevent the Melville of *Moby-Dick* from adopting some of the conventions of Shakespearean tragedy when he felt their relevance.

It is, of course, suggestive that Melville and Conrad share about

[9]"Some Techniques of Melville's Perception," in *Discussions of Moby-Dick*, ed. Milton R. Stern (Boston, 1960), p. 115.

as many techniques as they do themes — and the number of each is substantial. The thematic correspondences are perhaps the more apparent and include such prevailing concerns in both writers as the problems of egoism, self-delusion, and betrayal; the universality of evil; the inevitability of failure; the perils of isolation and withdrawal; the need for peace and the urge toward suicide; the danger of truth and the need of illusions; the hindrances to accurate perception; the confrontation with a hostile or indifferent world; and the dilemma of moral conduct. Paralleling many of these common themes are like techniques for conveying them. We find such narrative devices as multiple perspectives and the signal choice and handling of the narrator. And we encounter a whole host of other techniques similarly designed to create and maintain a suitable detachment from the subject — both the writer's and, as a consequence, the reader's also. Indeed, what Frederick Karl has said of Conrad with only mild exaggeration — that "all of [his] artistic devices, if they were to be listed categorically, would perhaps come together under the major classification of aesthetic distance or impersonality"[10] — is generally true of Melville as well. The more pointed of these distancing techniques would probably include such devices as controlled ambiguity, highly intellectualized rhetoric, formal and informal digressions, the deliberate fragmentation or discontinuance of episode, the open ending, and the sustained use of tonal irony (accompanied in certain novels and stories by the *mode* of irony as an overall structuring device).

Such devices can indeed be made to operate so effectively that the reader is left with no one in the narrative with whom he can identify and must therefore search in vain for anything like a hero. And unquestionably these techniques do tend toward the disappearance of the traditional protagonist. In Melville's work, for example, who can we confidently label the hero of "Bartleby," "Benito Cereno," *The Confidence-Man,* or *Billy Budd?* In Conrad's fiction, who can we point to as the main character of "Heart of Darkness,"

---

[10] *A Reader's Guide to Joseph Conrad* (New York, 1960), p. 18.

Nostromo, The Secret Agent, or *Chance*? The frequent employment of first-person narration has, further, the curious effect of placing the central subject midway between the protagonist and the narrator, who is in search of him. Beside "Bartleby" and "Heart of Darkness" (and, though not in a strict sense, "Benito Cereno" also), we might mention here as other examples of the "split center" *Moby-Dick, Lord Jim,* and "The Secret Sharer." In the end, all these devices make the reader not only less personally involved in the narrative, but also more skeptical, more reflective and critical about the meaning of it all. This situation explains why the reading of both authors is as much an intellectual experience as anything else and why only the film versions of their tales offer the entertaining diversion of rapidly paced physical adventure and empathy with some unequivocal hero.

Supplementing the various similarities between the two authors in content and form are the impressive resemblances to be found between their characters. Both Melville and Conrad tend to people their dramas with characters who are typical rather than unique, and a few major characters excluded, their dramatis personae is an assortment of different personality types. Such a circumstance is particularly evident in the two writers' maritime tales, and one advantage both authors saw in using the ship locale was that it provided a convenient microcosm for examining the diversities of human behavior in their most elemental manifestations. As we are told by the Ishmael-like narrator at the beginning of *Mardi:* "Now, at sea, and in the fellowship of sailors, all men appear as they are. No school like a ship for studying human nature."[11] To both authors, the rudimentary conditions aboard ship helped uncover man's fundamental impulses and enabled them to be commu-

---

[11]*Mardi* (London: Constable & Co., 1922-24), I.iii.16. All citations to this edition—as yet the standard one for Melville (though it will eventually be replaced by the definitive Northwestern-Newberry edition currently in progress)—will be incorporated in the text. For ease of reference generally, both chapter indications (represented by lower case roman numerals) and page numbers will be given. In cases where a novel is divided into two volumes (as the above), the volume number (represented by upper case roman numerals) will be given as well.

nicated to the reader with greater immediacy. To press this advantage, Melville and Conrad strove to make their crews representative of a variety of types. Conrad in *The Nigger of the "Narcissus"* calls attention to the heterogeneous nature of his crew, and Melville seems to have been obsessed with the microcosmic possibilities of a drama enacted on board ship. The miscellaneous crew of the *Pequod,* for example, is an "Anacharsis Clootz deputation from all the isles of the sea, and all the ends of the earth" *(M-D,* I.xxvii.149) and the assortment of riverboat passengers on the *Fidèle* in *The Confidence-Man* is designed to represent "all kinds of that multiform pilgrim species, man" (ii.9).

Since Melville and Conrad's vision of man's nature was, as this study aims to illustrate, very similar, it is hardly surprising that a number of characters in their narratives are closely comparable. Probably the two characters most spiritually akin are Ahab and Kurtz, their most compelling characters as well. Nevertheless, the great importance of the parallels between them makes it advisable to reserve discussion of them until the next chapter. One other especially notable character likeness is that between Pierre and Lord Jim. But since the affinities between them have mostly to do with overall conception, and since both represent a common literary type (the romantic egoist who quixotically follows his dream in defiance of all his surroundings), it might belabor the argument to dwell upon their basic similarities. One interesting link between them—their youthful admiration for Shakespeare—might be remarked upon, however. Pierre is undoubtedly a far more intellectual type than Jim, and the fact that Jim, whom we remember in part as an inarticulate stammerer, carries about a "half-crown complete Shakespeare"[12] effectively suggests the imaginative and idealistic depths of both questers.

---

[12]*Lord Jim* (New York: Doubleday, Page & Co., 1924), xxiii.237. All future references are to this central edition of Conrad's works and will be included parenthetically in the text by chapter and page (or by section, chapter, and page). Citations are titles (generally abbreviated) of original book publications, not of constituent stories.

The two sets of personages whose resemblances will be sketched here are less complex as individuals than Ahab and Kurtz, or Pierre and Jim, but taking a look at them may be useful in indicating how both writers were similarly impressed by certain human types. The first pair to be dealt with—James Wait of the *Narcissus* and Jackson, Redburn's intimidating shipmate on board the *Highlander*—are plainly products of the same dark mold. Both men have a natural disinclination for hard work and a history of shirking their duties on ship; both have learned the secret of oppressing their fellow-men with impunity; both stand in opposition to the two writers' values of fellowship and fidelity; and, finally, both are natural breeders of discord. Melville's treatment of Jackson (memorable even though it forms only a small fraction of *Redburn's* contents) and Conrad's handling of the Negro (who furnishes "the centre of the ship's collective psychology and the pivot of the action" [*Nigger*, p. ix]) reveal the two authors' tremendous fascination with the type. Three quotations—the first two from *Redburn*, the third from *The Nigger of the "Narcissus"*—should demonstrate the similarity of Melville and Conrad's interest in their moribund despots.

> They all stood in mortal fear of him [Jackson]; and cringed and fawned about him like so many spaniels. . .and used to watch, and tend, and nurse him every way. And all the time, he would sit scowling on them, and found fault with what they did. . . . (xii.75)

> Yet still in his tremulous grasp he swayed his sceptre, and ruled us all like a tyrant to the last. (lv.356)

> We served him in his bed with rage and humility, as though we had been the base courtiers of a hated prince; and he rewarded us by his unconciliating criticism. . . . He made himself master of every moment of our existence. (ii.37)

These passages disclose a fundamental affinity in what struck the authors as significant; their scrutinizing eye tended not only to fix itself upon the same sight but to extract much the same lesson from the spectacle as well.[13] It was not, we might add, a lesson either was inclined to forget. There is something of Wait in the dying yet overbearing Kurtz, whose voice continues to ring, like the Negro's, both "hollow and loud" *(Nigger,* ii.35); and even in Queequeg, Melville's noblest of savages, the oncoming (or rather, *suspected* oncoming) of death transforms the kind-hearted cannibal into a veritable dictator. Having ordered his aquatic deathbed in advance, he imperiously insists that the coffin be brought to him — "nor," as Ishmael comments, "was there any denying him; seeing that, of all mortals, some dying men are the most tyrannical" *(M-D,* II.cx.248).

The pugnacity and perversity of such dying men as Jackson and Wait is best observed in the way they react to their fellow creatures. It will be recalled how generously the Negro responds to the lowly, cadging Donkin, who in his hardened cynicism has alone among the crew no compassion to spare for him. Even though Donkin constantly accuses Wait of malingering, the otherwise intolerant Negro reacts to him at one point by lending him a jersey and at another by giving him a couple of old sea boots. On the other hand, the Irish sentimentalist Belfast, who is most solicitous of all toward him — even putting himself in jeopardy by stealing for him the officers' Sunday fruit pie — is constantly derided by the Negro. This wayward behavior exactly parallels the contrariness of Jackson, who seems to recognize as kindred spirits those who are least concerned about his physical state. We are told that "those who did the most for him, and cringed the most before him, were

---

[13]Jay Leyda, in *The Melville Log,* II (New York, 1951), 861, drops Conrad's name as one "certainly touched off" by Melville. Such an assumption not only can be shown to be untenable, but also misses by its very nature the main point in the relationship between the two writers: namely, that both were "touched off" by the same thing. On the other hand, when in a footnote Conrad biographer Jocelyn Baines specifically equates Jackson and Wait in their tyrannical and tubercular natures, he feels obliged to add that such similarities "are almost certainly a coincidence" *(Joseph Conrad: A Critical Biography* [London, 1960], p. 77). Still, while on one level his conclusion is sound and appropriately cautious, Conrad's so similar *regard* for a similar type of character does not deserve dismissal as merely coincidental.

the very ones he most abused; while two or three who held more aloof, he treated with a little consideration" *(Redburn,* xii.75). Undoubtedly, the two sailors are natural bullies, and the psychology underlying their behavior, it should be obvious, is comprehended in the same terms by both authors.

The second pair of characters who lend themselves to a joint consideration are two obtuse but successful Captains: Melville's Captain Delano and Conrad's Captain Mitchell in *Nostromo.* Through them, both authors dramatize their unhappy awareness of the inverse relationship between perspicacity and good fortune. Providence seems to be precisely with those who have the most unjustifiable faith in it. And the very dullness of perception that encourages the two Captain's imperturbable belief in their security operates uncannily to insure it. Both men represent a type the two authors viewed ambivalently: the man who is recognizably good and therefore merits a favorable estimation, yet whose naive conception of life is deserving of the most rigorous criticism, even contempt. The two writers' sense of mental superiority to such individuals may be discerned in the patronizing tone used to describe them. It will be observed that the portrayal of Mitchell below is essentially accurate as a description of Delano, and its implied judgment of the type should suggest Melville and Conrad's common angle of vision:

> The old sailor, with all his small weaknesses and absurdities, was constitutionally incapable of entertaining for any length of time a fear of his personal safety. . . . Unfortunately, Captain Mitchell had not much penetration of any kind; characteristic, illuminating trifles of expression, action, or movement, escaped him completely. He was too pompously and innocently aware of his own existence to observe that of others. (III.ii.338)

Although this characterization hardly offers anything of a tribute to the man, the very pattern of action in the book (and in "Benito Cereno" also) somehow affirms the practical value of his blindness.

On the other hand, the characters toward whom Melville and Conrad typically show the most sympathy are far less triumphant in their actions. Broadly speaking, they are all examples of the isolated man. Melville gives us a succinct description of the type in *Moby-Dick* when he refers to the whalemen on the *Pequod* collectively as *Isolatoes*, "not acknowledging the common continent of men, but each *Isolato* living on a separate continent of his own" (I.xxvii.149). Knowing something of the feelings of isolation that beset Melville and Conrad themselves (and Conrad's sense of being "cut off" was especially acute), it is only logical that the two writers should have been preoccupied in their tale-telling with insular figures. And quite possibly it is here that we find the best explanation for their considerable sympathy toward the outlaw—a sympathy particularly noteworthy in Conrad, whose strong ethical commitments would otherwise seem to preclude any kinship of feeling toward him. But, like Melville, he could easily identify with the moral outcast, for he perceived him as one who pursued his dream without regard for conventional standards.

The prevalence of independent or isolated characters in the fiction of both writers is best evidenced by a simple enumeration of their occurrence. In Melville, examples include Taji, Redburn, White Jacket, Ishmael, Ahab, Isabel, the disillusioned Pierre, Israel Potter, Bartleby, the Confidence Man, and Claggart. In Conrad also, we are able to make a substantial catalogue of the type, and our list becomes, like the one on Melville, more intriguing by the differences of personality it encompasses. We may note such isolated or exiled figures as Almayer, Willems, Kurtz, Jim, Yanko Goorall, Falk, the final Nostromo, Decoud, Mrs. Verloc, Razumov, Leggatt, Renouard (of "The Planter of Malata"), Heyst, Lena, Jones, Lingard, and Peyrol. Almost all of these characters, either by temperament or circumstance, are forced at some point to live apart from the human community. But as Melville and Conrad constantly demonstrate, the very nature of human existence makes it impossible for them to succeed in isolation. Especially worthy of mention here are the self-deluding idealists, who fall into isolation while striving to rise above their natural selves. Their intensely personal ideas of "how to be" lead them ultimately to adopt an egoistic line of conduct that eventuates in their own destruction — and often (as in the cases of Ahab and Pierre, or Kurtz and Jim) in the destruction of others as well. So aware are the two authors of the dangers of the independent self that while they may naturally sympathize with the outsider, their consciousness of his personal inadequacies makes them both finally critical of him.

If Melville and Conrad can be described as ambivalent toward their "isolatoes," their attitude toward the women in their fiction may be defined in general as positively hostile. Such a view may at first seem disputable, for examples do exist that would appear to support an opposite standpoint: that is, both authors show a common tendency to idealize or sentimentalize their feminine creations. In Melville, we may recall the Fayaway of *Typee,* the Yillah of *Mardi,* and the almost explicitly angelic Lucy of *Pierre.* In the somewhat less male-dominated world of Conrad, we may think of more examples: there is Kurtz's Intended, Jewel, Emilia Gould, Nathalia Haldin, Flora de Barral, Lena, and Doña Rita (in *The Arrow of Gold).* But beneath this romanticization of the sex there seems to lurk a deep-seated mistrust, rooted in the threat women pose not only to man's inner peace and contentment, but at times to his very existence. However unintentionally, Yillah and Isabel drive Taji and Pierre toward their deaths. In Conrad, too, the seductress is altogether familiar (though limited almost exclusively to the author's minor works). There is Nina in *Almayer's Folly,* Aissa in *An Outcast of the Islands,* Matara's sister in "Karain," Arsat's woman in "The Lagoon," Doña Erminia in "Gaspar Ruiz," Freya in "Freya of the Seven Isles," Felicia Moorsom in "The Planter of Malata," and Mrs. Travers in *The Rescue.* And even Amy Foster, a woman whose compassionate nature and stolid mind would appear to make her the most harmless sort, can, by the very narrowness of her understanding, be held responsible for the pathetic death of Yanko, her abandoned husband. The conclusion to be reached here, I think, is that the misogyny latent in both authors (and in Conrad not really so latent at all) is attributable to the menace that woman presented in her often irresistible sexual attraction. By dint of an enticing femininity she might decoy man into the snare of passion and consequently endanger the clarity of judgment upon which he depended for survival as a respectable human being.

By now enough should have been said about the affinities between Melville and Conrad for the reader to feel the need of more elaboration on Conrad's professed antipathy for the American author. We know about Conrad's feelings mainly from his unwillingness to write an introduction to a new edition of *Moby-Dick* planned by Oxford Press. In his polite but firm letter of refusal, he remarked: "Years ago I looked into *Typee* and *Omoo,* but as I didn't find there what I am looking for when I open a book I did go no further. Lately I had in my hand *Moby Dick.* It struck me as a rather strained rhapsody with whaling for a subject and not a single sincere line in the 3 vols of it."[14] Such crotchety remarks as these do not really help very much to account for Conrad's hostility toward Melville. And so if we are to clarify his curious aversion for a kindred creative spirit, it will be necessary to investigate just what in the author's work must have alienated him.

Most obvious among the factors for Conrad's dislike of Melville would be his understandable fear of being linked with a writer known primarily not for his artistic skill but for his "sea stuff." Throughout his writing career Conrad reaffirmed his serious intent, and his troubled reflections suggest how he must have reacted when asked to join his name with Melville's, whose reputation was then fundamentally as a talented weaver of adventures. To Sir Sidney Colvin, Conrad once wrote: "Perhaps you won't find it presumption if, after 22 years of work, I may say that I have not been very well understood. I have been called a writer of the sea, of the tropics, a descriptive writer, a romantic writer—and also a realist. But as a matter of fact all my concern has been with the

---

[14]Letter to Mr. Humphrey Milford, 15 January 1907, printed (along with a comment by Frank MacShane in *American Literature,* XXIX (1957-58), 463-464.

'ideal' values of things, events, and people. That and nothing else."[15] And a year before his death he wrote to Richard Curle: "I may have been a seaman, but I am a writer of prose. Indeed, the nature of my writing runs the risk of being obscured by the nature of my material.[16] Deploring his common designation as a sea writer, Conrad was naturally inclined to denounce an author whose name immediately evoked the picture of a romantic maritime adventurer. And while Conrad could generously pay homage in his essays to such nautical novelists as Cooper and Marryat, he must have viewed Melville, much closer to him in time and temperament, as constituting a very real threat to the image of himself he wished to cultivate. This circumstance may well explain the fact that Conrad never even deigns to allude to Melville in any of his volumes of nonfiction prose.

If Melville was known as a writer of sea yarns, he was also recognized, by virtue of his first two books, as an exoticist. Since Conrad knew both *Typee* and *Omoo* firsthand, and since his own first pair of works, *Almayer's Folly* and *An Outcast of the Islands*, were also exotic in subject, we should be able to appreciate his anxiety at having them placed alongside Melville's romanticized documentaries. Conrad's defensive attitude toward the exoticism popularly attributed to his first creative efforts is suggested in the preface he wrote to *An Outcast* for the collected edition of his works many years later. Reminiscing on that novel's reception, he observed: "though it brought me the qualification of 'exotic writer' I don't think the charge was at all justified. For the life of me I don't see that there is the slightest exotic spirit in the conception or style of that novel" (p. ix). On the other hand, there *is* an "exotic spirit" in *Typee* and *Omoo*, where savage life is frequently idealized in the manner of a Rousseau. And whereas Melville in his youthful primitivistic leanings may have tended to praise uncrit-

[15]18 March 1917, in G. Jean-Aubry, *Joseph Conrad: Life and Letters*, II (London, 1927), 185.

[16]14 July 1923, in *Conrad to a Friend*, ed. Richard Curle (London, 1927), p. 185.

ically the purity of his Polynesian subjects, Conrad, from the very belated start of his literary career, showed himself obsessed with the idea of man's innate corruption. Much more ironically detached from his characters than the early enthusiastic Melville, he was far more skeptical of their motives. And more widely experienced with the pettiness and stupidity of uncivilized people, he must have regarded Melville's attraction for the Polynesians' apparent innocence as naive self-delusion.

Not only was it natural for Conrad to feel a certain repugnance for an author whose settings might imply false parallels to his own work, but also the form (or lack of it) in the Melville he knew must have been intolerable to him. Deeply influenced by the craft of such authors as Flaubert, Maupassant, and James, he was annoyed by novelists who gave way to their undisciplined impulses. Writing of the "national English novelist," Conrad once described his typical production as an "instinctive, often unreasoned, out-pouring of his own emotions." For he did not—as Conrad took such care to—construct his book dispassionately and with a clear purpose (see *Last Essays*, p. 132). Such a belittlement of the traditional Anglo-Saxon novelist is indicative of what must have been Conrad's response to Melville's highly discursive South Sea books, as well as to his heterogeneous "whaling rhapsody." Add to this Melville's tremendous allusiveness and display of learning (which the intellectually modest Conrad must have regarded mostly as pedantry), and the fact that the language in *Moby-Dick* is at times emotionally overcharged by rhetoric admittedly "unnatural," and we can understand, further, Conrad's seemingly eccentric remark that Melville's whaling book had not a "single sincere line" in it. For Conrad was self-consciously dedicated to the faithful portrayal of the external world, and the romantically erratic elements so apparent in *Moby-Dick* could not but have disturbed his aesthetic sense.

A corollary to Conrad's imperatives on creative control was the notion that if books were to attain the level of art, they were disqualified from having any didactic content. His sometime collaborator, Ford Madox Ford, made this viewpoint plain when he observed that both Conrad and himself were agreed that as a serious practitioner of the novel "the one thing that you can not do is to propagandise, as author, for any cause. You must not, as author, utter any views. . . ."[17] Looking at Melville, as author, we may note the abundant propagandizing in both *Typee* and *Omoo* on the European corruption of uncivilized innocents and the wrongheadedness of the missionaries. Although these books never really aspire to the novel form, Conrad's aversion for explicit moralizing and essaylike digression in an essentially narrative work may well account for his remark that he did not find in *Typee* and *Omoo* what he looked for in reading a book. In *Moby-Dick,* too, Conrad must have found cause for impatience in Ishmael's tendency to become disembodied and to render, "as author," judgments on the narrative.

Melville's "portentous mysticism"—a phrase used by Richard Curle in his memoirs of Conrad to account for the writer's disparagement of the author of *Moby-Dick*[18]—was, of course, also at war with Conrad's ideas on the novelist's function. Distrusting science and philosophy alike, he felt the literary artist should devote himself to accurate (though suggestive) renderings of empirical reality. The endless speculations of *Moby-Dick*—its ponderings over God and the moral nature of the universe, and its reflections on fate and free will—all must have exasperated an author who denied the novelist the privilege of exploiting his fictional material for purposes of philosophical exploration. The metaphysical pursuit that gives *Moby-Dick* its essential form also must have irritated the sensibilities of one who, like his own Winnie Verloc in *The Secret Agent,* "felt profoundly that things do not stand much looking into" (viii.177). Conrad could not have had much sympathy with Melville's urge to dramatize the undramatizable: to revolve his narrative around a madman whose quest for what he himself perceives as "inscrutable" must, by definition, be futile. In fact, he

---

[17]*Joseph Conrad: A Personal Remembrance* (London, 1924), p. 208. See also Conrad's *Chance,* pp. xi-xii.

[18]*The Last Twelve Years of Joseph Conrad* (New York, 1928), p. 108.

was apt to regard such subjects as "insane" themselves. The criticism of Dostoevsky implicit in a laudatory essay he once wrote on Turgenev should suggest his reaction to Ahab. Writing of the very human nature of Turgenev's creations, he pointedly remarked that they were not "damned souls knocking themselves to pieces in the stuffy darkness of mystical contradictions" *(Notes on Life and Letters*, p. 47). Surely Ahab, who rebelliously seeks to "strike through the mask" that is the white whale, likewise does injury to himself and to his humanity. For an author to identify so closely with a figure ultimately so demonic must have disturbed Conrad, who was at once less bold a writer and a far more ethically committed one. As he commented in an essay entitled "Books": "It must not be supposed that I claim for the artist in fiction the freedom of moral Nihilism" *(Notes on Life and Letters*, p. 8). He held that certain ethical standards were crucial to civilized existence, and however illusory he might in his most lucid moments have realized these standards to be, he was frightened by a writer who would dare put their arbitrariness to the test. For the radical lawlessness promoted by such an investigation of life's "heart of darkness" might, he suspected, eventuate in the collapse of institutions man desperately required if he were to live in some semblance of peace and harmony.

No doubt Conrad's rigid sense of moral responsibility prevented him from recognizing that the author of *Moby-Dick* was himself very critical of his monomaniacal hero. For though there are times when Melville's identification with Ahab may be very close, still, as Leon Howard has duly emphasized, the relationship is emotional, not ideological.[19] If the book is read disinterestedly, the author's final perspective emerges as much closer to Ishmael's — just as in "Heart of Darkness" Conrad's point of view is unquestionably to be linked with Marlow's rather than with the abandoned Kurtz. Yet the threat of nihilism in *Moby-Dick* is undeniable, and

[19]"Herman Melville: *Moby-Dick*," in *The American Novel*, ed. Wallace Stegner (New York, 1965), p. 33. See also Howard's *Herman Melville*, Univ. of Minnesota Pamphlets on Am. Writers, No. 13 (Minneapolis, 1961), p. 24.

Conrad (himself accused, to his chagrin, of being nihilistic in his early, most morally exploratory, works) could hardly be expected to acknowledge Melville's achievement, even to himself. The deep philosophic and ethical problems raised by Ahab's grand quest were, of course, familiar enough to the creator of such figures as Kurtz, Jim, Decoud, and Heyst. But even here Conrad's intellectual attitude tended toward strong disapproval. Feeling obliged to condemn everything that in its individuality might foster the anarchic, he consciously denied the logic of his most incisive probings into the nature of existence. His dislike for the author of *Moby-Dick*, therefore, is no proof that the American writer's sensibilities were alien to his own. For, as the following pages should show, the profound affinities between his work and Melville's offer so much evidence of their spiritual relationship that his very protestations to the contrary suggest more than anything else the great barriers that may divide an author's public views from his deepest, most private vision of life.

CHAPTER I

EGOISM AND
THE CORRUPT NATURE OF MAN

Both Melville and Conrad show in their fiction an acute awareness of man's egoistic nature—an irremediable self-centeredness that contaminates his actions and predetermines his failure whenever he presumes to elevate himself above the moral status quo of society. Probably the most emphatic examples of man's inherent egoism to be found in their work are the ambitiously idealistic and "potentially" superior Ahab and Kurtz. An initial discussion of the impressive similarities between them should thus be useful in suggesting their creators' general incredulity about man's capacity for selfless, untainted heroism.

The most obvious parallel between Ahab and Kurtz is that both are gifted men. Such a description has far more to do with their exceptional personal qualities than with any moral excellence, since a gifted person is not necessarily a good one. It may, in fact, be quite the contrary. As the disenchanted Tekla in Conrad's *Under Western Eyes* says of the revolutionary, Peter Ivanovitch: "He is a great man. Great men are horrible" (III.ii.232). And Marlow, even after gaining full insight into the frightful darkness of Kurtz's soul, can speak of that immensely talented man as a "universal genius" *(Youth and Two Other Stories,* iii. 154). The actual goodness of an Ahab or Kurtz remains hypothetical: the Captain's pursuit of the inscrutable malice he sees in the leviathan who has torn off his leg may be little more than an insane rationalization of his lust to be revenged; Kurtz's professed humanitarian zeal may have been from the start only a lame excuse for his materialistic drive and demagogic craving to subjugate others.

But, for better or worse, both men possess the personal magnetism requisite for shaping the responses of others. Ahab can inspire the crew of the *Pequod* with an unholy passion for the blood of his deadly foe, and Kurtz is able to mold the natives in his station into tools whereby he may mercilessly extract the more ivory. As Marlow tells us: "Whatever he was, he was not common. He had the power to charm or frighten rudimentary souls into an aggravated witch-dance in his honour" (*MD*, ii.119). Captain Peleg's portrayal of Ahab reveals the same type of extraordinary personality. To Peleg, the *Pequod's* sovereign officer is a "grand, ungodly, godlike man" who is "above the common" and who (even more coincidentally) has "been in college, as well as 'mong the cannibals" (I.xvi.99).

Unfortunately, the very considerable gifts of both men are ultimately at the service of an uncontrollable egoism. Their persuasive rhetoric and overbearing manner enable them to manipulate others as might an unscrupulous hypnotist, and so skilled are they at getting others to believe what they wish them to that an exaggerated belief in their own worth soon prompts them toward acts at once irresponsible toward society and to their better selves. Both Melville and Conrad are explicit about their protagonist's extravagant self-regard. The egoism of Ahab inevitably merges into willful solipsism when he observes his riveted doubloon and can see only himself in it. Studying the profusely stamped gold coin, he remarks to himself: "There's something ever egotistical in mountain-tops and towers, and all other grand and lofty things; look here, —three peaks as proud as Lucifer. The firm tower, that is Ahab; the volcano, that is Ahab; the courageous, the undaunted, and victorious fowl, that, too, is Ahab; all are Ahab" (II.xcix.190). If the outer world exists for the crazed Captain, it is only because it has been deflated and then engulfed by his voracious self. Even the objective reality of his fellow-men eventually disappears as he comes to perceive them as extensions of his own being, catering to the demands of his will. Addressing the men in his boat on the last day of the chase, he tells them: "Ye are not other men, but my arms and legs; and so obey me" (II.cxxxv.361).

The egoism of Kurtz likewise leads to a cruel and dangerous distortion of perspective once that obsessed rhetorician can no longer recognize the discrete identity of anything outside himself. His ungovernable sense of possession breaks down his ability to distinguish between what he can own and what he as mortal can merely relate to. Marlow, both fascinated and awed by the demonism of such an attitude, remarks: "You should have heard him say, 'My ivory.' Oh yes, I heard him. 'My Intended, my ivory, my station, my river, my —' everything belonged to him. . . . Everything belonged to him — but that was a trifle. The thing was to know what he belonged to, how many powers of darkness claimed him for their own" (ii.116). Just as Ahab's egoism enthralls him to Fedallah, the Parsee harpooner whom Melville employs to embody his demonized self, so does Kurtz's radical self-centeredness transfigure him into one of "the devils of the land." By way of demonstrating the tenability of transferring critical comments made about one author (or his characters) to another with the same kind of creative imagination, we might reproduce here Richard Chase's incisive interpretation of Melville's unbridled Captain, keeping in mind its special relevance to Kurtz. "To be Ahab," Chase observes, "is to be unable to resist the hypnotic attraction of the self with its impulse to envelop and control the universe."[1]

Once such characters as Ahab and Kurtz have lost all sense of society, the central threat to their welfare comes not from without but from within. Made fearless by a self that has ceased to acknowledge the legitimate existence of others, they act with a recklessness that must end in self-defeat. This is what Starbuck has in mind when he dares warn his determined Captain "not to beware of Starbuck; thou wouldst but laugh; but let Ahab beware of Ahab; beware of thyself, old man" (II.cix.244). The paradox here is that

[1] *The American Novel and Its Tradition* (New York, 1957), p. 108.

Ahab creates the conditions for his defeat precisely in his dogged refusal to consider its possibility. With the loss of personal restraint, he also loses his one defense against a hazardous and potentially overpowering universe. Heeding nothing but his insatiable will, he falls victim to it. And it is the same with Kurtz, who, because he cannot restrain his drives, becomes "a tree swayed by the wind" (ii.119).

More and more the grandiose illusions that the two characters have about the nature of their missions are exposed as perilous self-delusions. Ahab conveniently ascribes all evil to the white whale and views his pursuit as a superhuman effort to rid the world of the leviathan's presence. But Melville, who knows all too well that every man harbors evil potentialities and that innocence is presumption, takes pains through his imagery to associate Ahab with the supposedly malevolent whale. He calls attention to Ahab's "ribbed and dented brow" (I.xxxvi.199; see also I.xliv.247 and II.cxiii.259) in the same way that he continually emphasizes Moby Dick's wrinkled forehead. As a result, we must finally view the revengeful Captain ironically, as symbolic of the very thing he has vaingloriously appointed himself to destroy. On this level, he is no longer opposed to his malicious enemy but morally equivalent to him.

So also with Kurtz, who in his physical decay is virtually transformed into the object of his greedy pursuits. Despite the partial humanitarianism of his undertaking, his egoism and materialistic urge eventually erode the benevolence of his motives until all that remains is his unappeasable ivory-lust. Wishing us to see Kurtz as so much ivory himself, Conrad renders his depraved tyrant through the most pointed imagery. When Marlow looks at the moribund Kurtz, he imaginatively sees "an animated image of death carved out of old ivory" (iii.134); and when he last gazes upon the expiring man, the creamy-white hue of the substance provides the shading for his bleakest portrait of all: "I saw on that ivory face the expression of sombre pride, of ruthless power, of craven terror—of an intense and hopeless despair" (iii.149).

The monstrous egoism of Ahab and Kurtz, which enables them to accommodate everything to their master passion, eventually leads—as seen by both authors—to madness. This madness may be camouflaged by eloquence, but it is nevertheless recognizable, for it results in compulsive acts that belie everything to which the two characters believe themselves idealistically devoted. There may even be rare moments when they have a glimpse of the perverted nature of their actions, but however much they may then loathe them, they are yet driven men and cannot abandon them. Needless to say, Melville and Conrad are aware that their heroes are not really mad in the traditional sense. It is, rather, that their reason has become focused exclusively on the all-absorbing self. Conrad's insight in his early story "An Outpost of Progress" on the "wrong-headed lucidity which may be observed in some lunatics" (*Tales of Unrest*, ii.115) serves as a useful commentary not only on his later work but also on the peculiar disorder of Ahab. And Ishmael's own explanation of his Captain's monomania is likewise instructive: "in that broad madness, not one jot of his great natural intellect had perished. . . . If such a furious trope may stand, his special lunacy stormed his general sanity, and carried it, and turned all its concentrated cannon upon its own mad mark" (I.xli.231). When we proceed to Marlow's description of the spiritually unbalanced Kurtz, we can hardly help having the illusion that the narrator has somehow conferred with Ishmael (his fictional cousin, as it were) before deciding how best to account for his subject's derangement. "Believe me or not," he tells his auditors, "his intelligence was perfectly clear—concentrated, it is true, upon himself with horrible intensity, yet clear. . . . But his soul was mad" (iii.144-145).

A "mad soul" to Conrad is surely an evil one, and it is not surprising that Melville, too, comes to view his deranged hero as demonic. The reasoning behind this essentially naturalistic—and psychologically convincing—theory of demonism is best explained by Marlow in his comment on the dying Brown in *Lord Jim*. Here he observes the kinship between madness and evil by pointing out how both are "derived from intense egoism" and "inflamed by resistance," and how both end by "tearing the soul to pieces" (xxxvii.344). Whether or not the idea of a mangled soul be clinically acceptable, it cogently translates into artistic terms the ethical dimensions of a dispossessed mind. For once the superego has capitulated to the id, the ego consciousness (i.e., the responsible soul) is irreparably mutilated. And the id for both authors is not simply an unknown quantity of instinctual energy but a definitely evil force. To Melville it is incarnated in the devilish figure of a Fedallah; to Conrad it is embodied in all the "powers of darkness." Such a complete loss of conscience can lead only to acts of brutal inhumanity. Ahab, without experiencing any self-reproach, can demonically beguile his crew into an unnecessary death; Kurtz, while continuing to assert the greatness of his plans, can heartlessly tyrannize and even sacrifice the natives whom he had originally aimed to assist. The "unextinguishable gift of noble and lofty expression," which Marlow tells us remains till the end with the voice that is Kurtz (iii. 147)—and which also describes the ever-eloquent Ahab, who goes down to defeat only after a final oratorical outburst —hardly makes either character impress us at last as very "noble and lofty" in conduct. Doubtless, Melville conceived of his Captain in far more heoric terms than did Conrad his megalomaniac, but the egoism underlying Ahab's almost superhuman courage throws into everlasting doubt his ultimate human value.

This investigation of the personalities of Ahab and Kurtz should make it clear that not simply the "villains" in Melville and Conrad exemplify the baser aspects of man. Indeed, almost *all* their major characters deserve to be seen as morally contaminated. For to be self-centered is only to be human, and as long as man is driven primarily by the instinct of self-gratification, he is qualified, according to the dictates of his temperament, for some villainous act or other. To quote once again Conrad's disillusioned but discerning Tekla: "a belief in a supernatural source of evil is not necessary; men alone are quite capable of every wickedness" (*UWE*, II.iv.151). And in *Nostromo*, Conrad, speaking in his own voice, remarks:

"At no time of the world's history have men been at a loss how to inflict mental and bodily anguish upon their fellow-creatures" (III.iv.373). In the end, man has mostly himself to blame for the omnipresence of evil, and to consign it all to some imaginary whale is willfully and irresponsibly to turn one's back on its human sources.

If Melville and Conrad were to have made manifest the negative potential of all their characters, however, they would have been both unfair to man and unrealistic about the nature of their world. Fortunately, because of the restraints and checks to which the majority of men are subject throughout their lives, most of the human potential for despicable acts is never realized. All the same, although there may be many sympathetic, or even commendable, characters in the fiction of both authors, hardly any of them are handled without a certain amount of skepticism. As Douglas Hewitt has written of Conrad: "There is a potentially evil or discreditable side to the natures of all his central characters, a seed of corruption in all their idealism, a suspicion that all our most elevated feelings derive at bottom from the same root as the hunger of Falk which had to be satisfied by cannibalism."[2] Since examples of such men are widespread in the works of Conrad, there is little point in enumerating them. The mixed moral nature of Melville's chief personae is, owing to the occasionally mythic or inscrutable nature of their conception, somewhat more difficult to ascertain. But though one should be very hesitant about criticizing the motives of a Queequeg, Bartleby, or Billy Budd, he is on fairly sure ground when he questions the psychic forces that drive a Taji, Ahab, Pierre, Captain Delano, Captain Vere, or—to take the most extreme example— a Confidence Man.

One of the ways in which both authors suggest the disreputable potential of their more admirable creations is by finding doubles less ethically committed to serve as their alter egos. This technique is admittedly much more elaborate in Conrad than in Melville, who,

[2]*Conrad: A Reassessment* (Cambridge, 1952), p. 77.

having a more "pure" interest in the nature of evil, tended to abstract or isolate it in select "innately depraved" characters. Thus we find in his fiction such natural degenerates as Jackson in *Redburn*, Bland in *White Jacket*, Babo, the Confidence Man, and Claggart. Nevertheless, there are significant instances of character doubling in Melville. His employment of Fedallah to personify Ahab's demonism has already been alluded to, but his use of Ahab as a double for Ishmael also deserves note. This is not to imply that the amiable Ishmael is something other than the trustworthy narrator we have always felt him to be, but to hint that his capacity to identify with the novel's lawless protagonist illustrates his own impulse to manipulate his surroundings according to the demands of his will. Melville (and, indeed, Ishmael himself) is too honest not to admit the attraction an Ahab must have to all but the most passive mortals. We recall the famous passage that occurs after Ahab has had the crew ceremoniously drink spirits and then swear its allegiance to his deadly purpose:

> I, Ishmael, was one of that crew; my shouts had gone up with the rest; my oath had been welded with theirs; and stronger I shouted, and more did I hammer and clinch my oath, because of the dread in my soul. A wild, mystical, sympathetical feeling was in me; Ahab's quenchless feud seemed mine. With greedy ears I learned the history of that murderous monster against whom I and all the others had taken our oaths of violence and revenge. (I.xli.222)

Acknowledging his own inclinations toward savage and undisciplined behavior while at the same time confessing his alarm over them, Ishmael looks ahead to the narrator of "Heart of Darkness." Marlow, too, is frank enough to admit his relationship to the primitive in man. And this admission is made even before he meets the "de-civilized" Kurtz. For on his perilous trip to the Inner Station, he is made witness to the uninhibited rituals common to African cannibals and confesses his "remote kinship with this wild and passionate uproar" (ii.96). Though he feels tempted to deny it, he realizes that these natives cannot be dismissed as mere animals.

And so long as he is compelled to appreciate them in human terms, he must recognize the threat they pose to civilized man, who has managed through the centuries to soften the barbaric noises emanating from within him; for however tempered, the inner cacophony is never permanently resolved. When Melville, writing of John Paul Jones's ferocity in *Israel Potter*, is led to comment on "the primeval savageness which ever slumbers in human kind, civilised or uncivilised" (xi.82), he illustrates the same consciousness of man's bestiality. It is this honesty that enables a man as scrupulous as Marlow to sympathize with the depraved Kurtz and generously pronounce that man's final insight into "the horror" an ethical triumph. For Marlow, who must hold on to the "surface-truth" of things in order to maintain his balance in the face of such lawless abandonment, can understand in Kurtz's degeneration his own capacity to revert to savagery once circumstances emerge that render irrelevant all the regulations of civilized society.

If Marlow can identify himself with Kurtz, it is even easier for him to identify with Jim. Certainly Jim is—as Marlow fearfully points out—"too much like one of us not to be dangerous" (*LJ*, ix.106). In his cowardice and self-concern, he has proved himself capable of violating one of the most sacred codes of seamanship; yet he is no simple villain and this fact suggests his unsettling effect on such a right-minded man as Marlow. For if the narrator cannot deny his kinship with the young romantic, he must acknowledge his own capacity to betray society and his own ideals once forced (or, indeed, "betrayed") by events into an extreme position such as Jim's. Marlow has a worrisome sense of man's flawed nature and the main reason he becomes so absorbed in Jim's fate is that he desperately needs to find some redeeming excuse for him— and thus for all men. In his many endeavors to help the youth we see his own felt necessity to expiate the guilt that, despite all his righteousness, he continues to recognize in himself. The "mystery and terror" (v.51) he sees in the fatal turn of events that has left Jim forever branded drives him to confront his own darker self and, indirectly, seek atonement for it. In a sense, this feeling of blame also accounts in Melville's "Bartleby" for the narrator-attorney's involvement with his spiritually shattered scrivener. All his attempts to appease his unidentifiable guilt by helping Bartleby having failed, he is finally led to exclaim: "Ah, Bartleby! Ah, humanity!" (*The Piazza Tales*, p. 65), recognizing his essential tie with the isolated and forever obstinate copyist. The lamenting tone here belongs to Marlow as well, for Conrad's narrator, too, must grieve over the fact that the fallible Jim is, irrefutably, "one of us."

To add further support to this notion that Jim is "the secret sharer" of what all apparently responsible men harbor within their deepest selves, Conrad presents us in the same novel with still another principled Captain forced to acknowledge the Jim in himself. This is Captain Brierly, described by Marlow as having enjoyed a career without blemish and without cause for self-doubt. But the eminently successful Captain who serves as juror in Jim's case is able to see in the young idealist before him his own abundant possibilities for moral failure. Like Marlow, he sees in Jim's transgression his terrifying culpability, but, unlike him, he is incapable of living with it. When his conceited regard for himself as a perfectly dependable and wholly incorruptible officer dissolves, he must foreclose the risks of his vulnerability by suicide. The more phlegmatic Marlow, naturally predisposed toward skepticism of every man's motives, including his own, is much better able to cope with his jarring insight into man's common guilt. Fortified by a more critical view of human nature, he can look on at Jim's spectacle disturbed but without a blush—as he has told us he witnessed savage rites in that other tale of man's pathetically flawed nature. And as he informs Jewel (who cannot understand why her noble protector has been found unworthy to live among his own people), though it may be true that Jim is not good enough, neither is, strictly considered, anyone else. His final words to her: "Nobody, nobody is good enough" (xxxiii.319), reveal unambiguously his humble opinion of the human creature.

This opinion is one with which Conrad, his equally skeptical creator, would concur fully. In a letter written to R. B. Cunninghame Graham just three months before the composition of *Lord Jim*, Conrad remarked to his idealistic friend: "Into the noblest causes, men manage to put something of their baseness. . . . Every cause is tainted: and you reject this one, espouse that other one as if one were evil and the other good, while the same evil you hate is in both, but disguised in different words."[3] This is why character doubling is no rare phenomenon in Conrad's fiction, and why—to give three more prominent examples of his use of it—the rehabilitated Jim is mysteriously linked to the villainous Brown, the Captain in "The Secret Sharer" is identified with the dangerously impulsive Leggatt, and the compassionate though detached Heyst is equated at various points with the devilish Jones.

Just as we may assume that the critical Marlow is, in his conviction that nobody is good enough, a spokesman for his creator, we may, I think, see one of Melville's most skeptical personae as that author's mouthpiece. The character in mind here is the cynical barber in *The Confidence-Man*, who, on being told by the wily swindler that he is shaving a philanthropist, responds: "I sadly fear, lest you philanthropists know better what goodness is, than what men are" (xliii.307). In both Melville and Conrad we may detect the same deeply distrustful attitude toward human nature, an attitude that leads in their novels to a close scrutiny of the actual goodness of their "better" characters' motives. What finally compromises the ethical worth of all man's actions is, as has already been said, the egoism all too perceptible behind them. Conrad himself is often explicit in communicating his ideas on the fundamental selfishness discernible in even the most seemingly altruistic behavior. In *Nostromo*, he allows Decoud ("incorrigible in his scepticism") to reflect of the title character that "this man was made incorruptible by his enormous vanity, that finest form of egoism which can take on the aspect of every virtue" (II . viii.300). Such a description is surely relevant to Melville's conception of

---

[3]February, 1898, in *Life and Letters*, I, 229.

Amasa Delano, a person whose generosity toward the unfortunate Don Benito and his ship is revealed at various points to be motivated largely by conceited self-righteousness and pride. Delano's feelings upon preparing to leave the ship of the apparently unappreciative Cereno clearly point to the vanity underlying his virtue. We are told that while waiting for his boat "a sort of saddened satisfaction stole over Captain Delano, at thinking of the kindly offices he had that day discharged for a stranger. Ah, thought he, after good actions one's conscience is never ungrateful, however much so the benefited party may be" (*The Piazza Tales*, pp. 139-140). If Delano is as good as he is, Melville seems to say, it is because his acting virtuously conveniently enhances his self-esteem. For him, doing good is far more gratifying than doing ill: ethically considered, he is merely fortunate in having a nature that thrives on the self-flattery earned by "selfless" behavior.

If we look ahead to *The Confidence-Man*, written shortly after "Benito Cereno," we can recognize the essence of the honorable Captain in the account Melville gives us of the "gentleman with gold sleeve-buttons," whose unstained (because untried) virtue cannot be doubted. After an elaborate description of his spotless person, the narrator sums him up simply as "one whose very good luck it was to be a very good man" (vii.47). The author, it appears, has much too keen a sense of man's self-interested nature to allow him to regard anyone as wholly admirable. Since one can never abandon his ego, he can never act disinterestedly. The attorney-narrator of "Bartleby" may at times seem commendable in his concern for, and even devotion to, his no longer productive copyist, but he is himself led to confess the element of egoism beneath his seeming noble-mindedness. While he may reflect considerably that firing Bartleby might jeopardize that inert man's future welfare, he is also busy weighing the benefits of keeping his scrivener. By allowing Bartleby to stay in his office, he observes unabashedly, he may "cheaply purchase a delicious self-approval"; such an act will enable him to "lay up in my soul what will eventually prove a sweet morsel for my conscience" (*The Piazza Tales*, p. 34). And later, when the situation with the immovable Bartleby becomes more desperate and he is at a loss regarding what move to take, he asks himself: "—you will not thrust such a helpless creature out of your door? you will not dishonour yourself by such cruelty?" (p. 55). At no point can he think of Bartleby's plight in itself: he must forever be estimating the cost of his benevolence. If he emerges, nonetheless, as more charitable than most, his goodness must be attributed not to any deeply felt philanthropy but to an all-encompassing pragmatism. A businessman in everything, he tells us quite as much himself by noting: "Aside from higher considerations, charity often operates as a vastly wise and prudent principle — a great safeguard to its possessor" (p. 52).

The egoism at the root of the lawyer's pity is comparable to the compassion the crew of the *Narcissus* feels toward the dying Wait. What is most interesting here is that Conrad not only perceives the shipmates' pity for the Negro as shallow, but also regards their charitable sentiments as dangerous, altogether capable of disrupting the order and discipline necessary for the well-being of the ship. The keynote is struck when we are informed that the sailors' concern for their moribund companion is essentially an expression of their own fear of death. Their irrational hope that Wait will somehow survive betrays their own cowardly need to delude themselves about their mortality. As the narrator puts it: "The latent egoism of tenderness to suffering appeared in the developing anxiety not to see him die" *(Nigger,* v.138). Since Conrad admires the traditional masculine values of courage, loyalty, endurance, and the like, and since he distrusts the more sentimentally charged values commonly regarded as feminine, it is understandable that he sees in the crew's sympathy for Wait a threat to what the orthodox-minded Marlow speaks of in *Lord Jim* as the "fidelity to a certain standard of conduct" (v.50). The self-indulgent aspects of the crew's compassion for the languishing Negro is given the sharpest emphasis: "He [Wait] was demoralising. Through him we were becoming highly humanised, tender, complex, excessively decadent: we understood the subtlety of his fear, sympathised with all his repulsions, shrinkings, evasions, delusions — as though we had been overcivilised, and rotten, and without any knowledge of the meaning of life" (v.139). Such a description can hardly be passed off as so much rhetoric either, for shortly before it occurs we are shown how close to mutiny the crew's abandoned feeling for Wait actually leads them. And when we are told how "falsehood triumphed" through the shipmates' sympathy for the dying Negro (v.138), and how Wait's death finally brings to the end their "sentimental lie" (v.155), we see how the author's unflinching view of the crew's conduct ultimately exposes the dishonorable egoism of their softer impulses.

The self-concern to be found in the mates' devotion toward the Negro parallels another form of pseudo altruism discernible in both writers. In mind here is the self-appointed savior of that favorite type traditionally known as "the fair maiden in distress." We think first of the knightly enthusiast, Pierre, who stakes all to rescue his half sister, Isabel. But however lofty his undertaking might at first appear, the very "fairness" of the damsel soon forces us to question whether the hero's motives in taking up her cause are as idealistic as he wishes to consider them. As Henry Murray has aptly put it in his psychoanalytic study of the book: "the hero believes he is motivated by Agape but, in truth, it is Eros that is impelling him."[4] For although Pierre may succeed in deluding himself about the grounds for his decision to befriend his ill-fated sister, the narrative very early reveals the depths of the physical allurement that has driven him to support her. Once again, apparent altruism emerges as essential egoism: Pierre's dominant concern is with the fulfillment of his own urgent masculine needs rather than with the fulfillment of any absolute fraternal commitments. It is not simply what he can do for Isabel, but what Isabel can do for him that determines him to link his fate recklessly with hers. Though in a more abstract sense, Taji's exaggerated concern with the fair Yillah in *Mardi* derives from the same roots.

[4]"Introduction" to *Pierre* (New York, 1962), p. ci.

In Conrad, we may note the same discrepancy between the professed and actual motives of the "gallant hero." Since Paul Wiley has already furnished us with a sharp delineation of the type, we can do no better than to quote him:

> Conrad provides an array of men of knightly appearance and lofty intention, like Anthony in *Chance*, Heyst in *Victory*, Renouard in "The Planter of Malata," and Lingard in *The Rescue*. What distinguishes all of these heroes is their readiness to assume the role of saviour, and in accordance with the chivalric tradition their aim is the rescue of a persecuted maiden or a lady whom they think it necessary to save. But although they are admirable for high qualities of idealism in the abstract, they find their vows troublesome in practice; for their ideals and visions are inspired by a heightened sensuality which Baudelaire would have understood far better than Galahad. Their quest ends in disaster or near disaster for the reason that their attempt at salvation of woman as a human being is confused with their pursuit of a phantasmal Aphrodite.[5]

Complementing the two authors' suspicions about man's ostensible virtue is their doubtfulness about the possibilities of social and political reform. Since man's egoistic nature is unchangeable, neither writer could hope for a future utopia. As Conrad pointed out to Cunninghame Graham: "You are misguided by the desire of the Impossible. . . . Alas! what you want to reform are not institutions, —it is human nature. Your faith will never move that mountain."[6] Conrad's disbelief in man's capacity for ethical rehabilitation finds its parallel in Melville—of whom biographer Newton Arvin has observed: "he had failed to find in history—or in his own experience—any warrant for a belief in human perfectibility."[7] Even in an early work such as *White Jacket*, which has as one of its aims the reform of abuses in the United States Navy, Melville felt obliged to add at the book's very conclusion: "Yet the worst

---

[5]*Conrad's Measure of Man* (Madison, Wisconsin, 1954), pp. 134-135.
[6]February, 1898, in *Life and Letters*, I, 229.
[7]*Herman Melville* (New York: Compass Books, 1957), p. 98.

of our evils we blindly inflict upon ourselves; our officers cannot remove them, even if they would" ([xciii].504). The greatest corruption of all, the author recognized, emanated from within each man's breast. This is why the worst of human ills were irreparable and why, also, Melville could never in good faith have made a career as a propagandist. For no institution, system of government, or society could remove evil so long as its chief source lay in man's unalterable egoism. Moving a year back to *Mardi*, we can easily decipher the ultimate meaning of the scroll discovered in Vivenza, which proclaims that "though all evils may be assuaged; all evils can not be done away. For evil is the chronic malady in the universe; and checked in one place, breaks forth in another" (II.lvii.244). The "chronic malady" here may be seen as referring to man's incurably selfish will and admits no remedy. It is Ahab's "inscrutable malice" brought down to the human level and accounts for man's enduring inhumanity.

If both writers tended toward the ironic rather than the satiric mode in their fiction, it is because although they may have disliked current social conditions, they had no faith in any alternatives. Melville's *Confidence-Man* may be satirical in temper but is hardly satirical in its ultimate purpose; and much the same is true of Conrad's *Secret Agent*. The extreme pessimism of a remark Conrad once made on crime surely accounts for his negative relationship to conventional satire: "Le crime est une condition nécessaire de l'existence organisée. La société est essentiellement criminelle, — ou elle n'existerait pas."[8] Such a bleak view of the human community may not be unlike that implicit in Melville's *Billy Budd*, where the very image of goodness must, it would seem, be sacrificed to preserve society. And while Melville the idealist might wish to condemn society for its own defensive condemnation of a Budd, his humane understanding of its basic necessities forbade him from doing so. Significantly, it is the utter *lack* of egoism in the young sailor that is hopelessly incompatible with the world's militancy,

[8]Letter to Cunninghame Graham, 8 February 1899, in *Life and Letters*, I, 269.

itself the product of man's corruptness. And so the execution of Budd had essentially to be understood as a sad affirmation of "criminal society." The common good, both Melville and Conrad regretfully came to realize, had very little to do with good at all. For it, too, was based on egoism. But, as Conrad himself immediately added to the letter just quoted, "C'est l'egoisme qui sauve tout, — absolument tout, — tout ce que nous abhorrons, tout ce que nous aimons. Et tout se tient."

CHAPTER II

SKEPTICISM:

THE STANCE OF DISILLUSIONMENT

The disillusionment resulting from the scrutiny of egoistic man in a society intrinsically corrupt represents only one aspect of Melville and Conrad's discouraged perspective of reality. Moving to the world outside man, they discovered far more cause for disenchantment. If man's inward peace was constantly endangered by the selfish interests of his fellowmen, his outward security was likewise threatened by a hostile universe.

The best symbol of this seemingly malevolent universe is, naturally enough, the mighty sea, which charmed and awed both writers and which provided the background for many of their most powerful dramas. To Melville and Conrad, the sea was no more deserving of trust than man. In *The Mirror of the Sea*, Conrad speaks of "its fascination that has lured so many to a violent death" (xxxv.136), and Melville has the same wary sense of its deceitfulness. In *Moby-Dick* he has Ishmael confront the reader with the unhappy situation in this fashion: "Consider the subtleness of the sea; how its most dreaded creatures glide under water, unapparent for the most part, and treacherously hidden beneath the loveliest tints of azure" (I.lviii.348). The sea's insidiousness is as inherent as man's depravity, and thus all attempts to "reform" its nature must be futile. Melville gives this idea special force in *Moby-Dick* by pointing out that "though but a moment's consideration will teach, that however baby man may brag of his science and skill, and however much, in a flattering future, that science and skill may augment;

yet forever and forever, to the crack of doom, the sea will insult and murder him, and pulverise the stateliest, stiffest frigate he can make" (I.lviii.347). Such a sentiment is clearly echoed in Conrad's remark that: "Unlike the earth, [the sea] cannot be subjugated at any cost of patience and toil" (*Mirror*, xxxv.136). The stubborn ferocity of the sea is a permanent condition, both authors seem to say, and one had better assume its hostility in advance. As Conrad warns: "To love it is not well" (*Mirror*, xxxvi.148). And if we remember the role it is given in such empirically based tales of Conrad's as *The Nigger of the "Narcissus,"* "Youth," *Lord Jim*, "Typhoon," and *The Shadow Line*, we realize that his avuncular advice is well founded. It makes no sense to be faithful to that which knows nothing of fidelity, and if the "unending menace" of the sea *(The Rescue*, II.vi.108) cannot be denied, its waters are best regarded as man's natural enemy.

This is not to say that the sea has any specific design in its heartlessness toward man. Both Melville and Conrad stress the complete arbitrariness of its destructive fury. When we are told in *Moby-Dick* that "the most terrific of all mortal disasters have immemorially and indiscriminately befallen tens and hundreds of thousands of those who have gone upon the waters" (I.lviii.347), we can appreciate how the sea is less monstrous than it is monstrously accidental. The point of its utter lack of discrimination in deciding upon its victims is sharpened even further when we are reminded how the sea is at odds not only with man — whom Melville views as alienated from it — but also with "the creatures which itself hath spawned." Even its noblest creature, the mighty whale, is handled with the same violent irreverence. Pitilessly dashed against the rocks, its corpse may be discovered lying alongside a shipwreck (I.lviii.348). Conrad is similarly struck by the "unfathomable cruelty" of the deep and, personifying the immortal foe of man, deplores its lack of generosity: "No display of manly qualities — courage, hardihood, endurance, faithfulness — has ever been known to touch its irresponsible consciousness of power" *(Mirror*, xxxvi.137).

The very haphazardness of the sea's malice makes both authors perceive it, finally, as not malicious at all but merely indifferent. To see it, and nature generally, as actively malevolent (as does Captain Ahab) is to delude oneself about its basic character. It is simply unconcerned with the welfare of those who travel upon it. Accountable only to its inherently amoral self, it is, as Conrad notes, "indifferent to good and evil" (*Mirror*, xxxvi.148). Even when Conrad, in *An Outcast of the Islands*, was at his most symbolistic in portraying nature, his lavish portraits hardly made it appear spiritually endowed. At one point, he speaks of the impartial river as "ready to carry friends or enemies, to nurse love or hate on its submissive and heartless bosom, to help or to hinder, to save life or give death; the great and rapid river: a deliverance, a prison, a refuge or a grave" (IV.i.214). At another point, focusing on the morally inert Malay jungle, he observes "the stolid impassiveness of inanimate things. . .[which] assert in their aspect of cold unconcern the high dignity of lifeless matter that surrounds, incurious and unmoved, the restless mysteries of the ever-changing, of the never-ending life" (IV.iii.242). In both cases we note the language of the symbolist and the perspective of the realist. For Conrad viewed nature as mechanical, not as some mystical organic process. As mechanism, it could hardly be seen as personally involved in man's destiny: hence its indifference to all his strivings and sufferings. It might witness the spiritual torture of a Don Benito and continue undisturbed its perpetual cycle of life and death. And when Captain Delano, urging his broken friend to put his woeful experience behind him, exclaims with unconscious irony: "See, yon bright sun has forgotten it all, and the blue sea, and the blue sky; these have turned over new leaves" (*The Piazza Tales*, p. 168), we are made to see not the soothing calm of nature but its callous unconcern.

From the two writers' disenchanted view of nature, it is only a small step to their skepticism regarding a benevolent Deity. For how might a responsible, solicitous God be the creator of a cosmos intrinsically menacing to man by its very indifference? This was a question neither Melville nor Conrad could answer, and it led both to agnosticism. With Conrad, naturally inclined toward unbelief, such a stance was easy enough to adopt, but for the far more religious-minded Melville it caused considerable restlessness. As Nathaniel Hawthorne in his journals once noted regretfully of his doubting and ever-speculating friend: "He can neither believe, nor be comfortable in his unbelief." Melville could place no certain faith in God because he could discover no comprehensible purpose in the universe of which, supposedly, He was Master. In consequence, the Deity appeared unconcerned with man's problems. By the time of *Moby-Dick*, Newton Arvin tells us, "In the traditional Christian God, the omniscient and loving Father, Melville had now lost all confident belief."[1] Insofar as he granted His presence at all, it was primarily as a force serving to define man's ceaseless struggles, a fact demonstrated most distressingly by the action of *Pierre*. Even Ishmael, whose faith seems capable of overriding endless doubts about the world's beneficence, perceives "a sort of interregnum in Providence" when at one point he recognizes his mortal welfare as wholly dependent upon Queequeg, to whom he is tied by a monkey-rope. His rationalization of a cosmic lapse is imperative if he is to cling to some belief that Providence is morally responsible and that, therefore, "its even-handed equity never could have sanctioned so gross an injustice" (II.lxxii.48). To begin to question the divine laws guiding man's destiny (and surely the author here is engaged in raising such doubts) is to move undeviatingly toward unbelief. If we move ahead to the skepticism everywhere implicit in *The Confidence-Man*, we can appreciate in one of the swindler's most astute remarks exactly where Melville's unfaltering rationalism had led him. "Set aside materialism," proposes the trickster, "and what is an atheist, but one who does not, or will not, see in the universe a ruling principle of love" (xxviii.178).

Conrad, too, was unable to detect any humanity in the heavenly forces governing man's fate. In his view, whatever God there was had somehow relegated His tasks to an impersonal universe, which

[1]*Herman Melville*, p. 190.

performed them with neither intelligence nor compassion. To use Conrad's adjectives in referring to the sea, the cosmic powers were at once "uncertain," "arbitrary," "featureless," "violent," "inane," "stupid," "persistent," "futile," and "wearisome" (*Notes on Life and Letters*, p. 184). A brief glance at three of the author's tales should make obvious his profound doubt in a benevolent Deity — or, for that matter, in any deity at all.

The four defective children who provide the title for the author's story "The Idiots" are described as "a reproach to empty heaven" (*Tales of Unrest*, p. 58). And their unfortunate mother cannot but proclaim after all her prayers have gone unanswered that: "There's no mercy in heaven — no justice" (p. 75). The theme of the untrustworthy Creator merges with that of an indifferent universe when at the close of the narrative, the mother, having hysterically jumped off a cliff into the sea, utters a cry for help, which seems "to dart upwards along the perpendicular face of the rock, and soar past, straight into the high and impassive heaven" (p. 84). It would seem that what motivated the author to write the story to begin with (and Conrad had actually seen the idiots) was his indignation at a world that could permit such tragedies to occur. In two other pathetic tales — "Amy Foster" and "The End of the Tether" — we find this same righteous anger at cosmic unconcern. The bitter irony in the lines that recount the pitiful death of the forsaken Yanko Goorall hardly need emphasizing. Left "sick — helpless — thirsty" by a dull, panicky wife, he is driven to confront his one friend, the physician-narrator, with man's ultimate question — and the response is predictable enough:

> "'Why?' he cried, in the penetrating and indignant voice of a man calling to a responsible Maker. A gust of wind and a swish of rain answered.
> "And as I turned away to shut the door he pronounced the word 'Merciful!' and expired." (*Typhoon and Other Stories*, p. 141)

The word that *we* are forced to pronounce, however, is "merciless," and it is a word evoked as well by the plight of Captain Whalley in

"The End of the Tether." Afflicted by blindness, the Captain is made to pay the full price for his "boundless trust in divine justice meted out to man's feelings on this earth" (*Youth*, xiv.324). Circumstances ultimately betray his baseless faith in Deity, and in the end he must acknowledge painfully—as does the arbitrarily accursed mother in "The Idiots"—that God has ignored all his pleas (see xiv.333).

If, then, Melville and Conrad were unable to justify confidence in nature or God (not to mention their fellowman), what might they legitimately believe in? One alternative was simply to believe in reason and abandon faith in everything else. But neither author could place much confidence in such behavior, for, paradoxically, their own reasonable appraisals of experience made it evident that one's reason was not to be trusted either. Too easily could it be swayed by passion into a line of thought having nothing whatsoever to do with rationality. As Marlow reflects in *Chance*: "the dreams of sentiment. . .are invincible. . . . It is never, never reason which governs men and women" (I.vii.206), and such a comment may remind us of Axel Heyst, none of whose major actions are justifiable in the light of his convictions. While reason might enable man to achieve the knowledge of self and society necessary to live as his nature required, both writers were well aware that in the end reason was powerless in controlling man's actions.

In Melville's *Pierre,* this notion of the final feebleness of one's thought finds expression in the narrator's observation that "there is no faith, and no stoicism, and no philosophy, that a mortal man can possibly evoke, which will stand the final test of a real impassioned onset of Life and Passion upon him" (XXI.ii.403). This disheartening insight accounts in one way or other for the eventual failure of most of the idealists in the two writers' fiction. It is especially helpful as a commentary on the fate of Heyst, who is also undone by following his romantic sentiments and running off with a forlorn—but beautiful—young woman. Indeed, Pierre and Heyst deserve to be placed side by side in the way they both misuse their rational faculties in order to lend support to impulses essentially unrelated to reason. Conrad's remark in *Victory* on his hero's false conception of his motives in deciding to take Lena away with him has quite as much bearing on the deliberations of Pierre. "The use of reason," he comments cynically, "is to justify the obscure desires that move our conduct, impulses, passions, prejudices and follies, and also our fears" (II.ii.83).

Not only were Melville and Conrad doubtful about the reasonableness of reason; they were also suspicious of its ethical value. Since reason might vindicate any action one wished to take, it could hardly be understood as having any ethical commitments. The behavior of Kurtz in the jungle may admit of the most eloquent explanations on his part, but it is nonetheless immoral. And Melville seems to have had a special awareness of reason's compatibility with "innate depravity." Very possibly he drew the connection through conceiving the devil as himself all intellect, gratified by the amorality of his endless plotting — here, at least, would appear to have been his inspiration for the demonic Confidence Man. And his idea of Claggart, whose self-composure and restraint would seem to suggest a person of some ethical sanity, is yet of one "having apparently little to do with reason further than to employ it as an ambidexter implement for effecting the irrational" (*BB*,x.46).

Skeptical of man and his reason on the one hand, and the universe and its benevolence on the other, Melville and Conrad had only one thing left in which they might put their trust. Every aspect of the world having failed to meet their prerequisites for faith, they naturally looked, as writers, to art — the direct antithesis of life — for a release from their prodigious skepticism. But even here they could discover no legitimate grounds for belief. For if art were to be worthy of trust, its ability to convey the truth was essential, and neither author could convince himself that art was equipped to carry out such a mission.

That both Melville and Conrad believed the primary aim of the artist was to convey the deep truths underlying appearances is abundantly evident. Melville, in his appreciative essay "Hawthorne and His Mosses," spoke enthusiastically of "Shakespeare and other masters of the great Art of Telling the Truth," and in his own works endeavored to uncover the most hidden truths of all. But he could never feel triumphant in his attempts to strike through the masks of reality. His prevailing distrust of philosophical systems—made manifest first in *Mardi*, where the discursive Babbalanja confesses himself in error for trying "to invest sublunary sounds with celestial sense" (II.x.37)—is complemented by a disbelief in the cognitive capacities of artistic expression. For, as Babbalanja proclaims, "truth is in things, and not in words" (I.xciii.329). So long as Melville recognized his fiction as "symbolic" (as, by its verbal nature, it had to be), he was compelled to see his writing as forever denied any dealings with truth. Despairing of the power of language to yield truth, he often felt obliged merely to present the reader with the "facts" of his imagination and leave him to interpret for himself any final truth implicit in them. Such an unassuming method of artistic construction is first pinpointed in *Moby-Dick* by Ishmael, who after conscientious attempts at portraying the sperm whale's face concludes by telling the reader that he must make what he can of it, for the narrator can do no more than place it before him (II.lxxix.83).

Melville's radical reservations about his art come to a head in *Pierre*, which ruthlessly exposes the pitiable vanity of the writer-hero's creative aspirations. Once again the fundamental discord between language and reality finds explicit statement in the author's bitter reflection that "when a man is in a really profound mood, then all merely verbal or written profundities are unspeakably repulsive, and seem downright childish to him" (XIV.i.288). The notion of the inescapable tendency of language toward facile definition constantly plagued Melville, who felt the impotence of literature in direct proportion to his pre-verbal intuitions of the truth. But even worse than the unbridgeable gap between art and veracity was literature's tidy contrivances, which ultimately dissolved all in artifice. In a key statement on the validity of Pierre's novel (which serves the double purpose of undermining the soundness of Melville's novel on Pierre), we are informed that

> the more and the more that he wrote, and the deeper and the deeper that he dived, Pierre saw the everlasting Elusiveness of Truth; the universal lurking insincerity of even the greatest and purest written thoughts. Like knavish cards, the leaves of all great books were covertly packed. He was but packing one set the more; and that a very poor jaded set and pack indeed. (XXV.iii.472)

Regarding the ineffectuality of literature in communicating truth, Conrad was never so explicit as the outspoken author of *Pierre*. Because he felt throughout his writing career that certain illusions had best not be questioned, he preferred to go on record as believing in art's essential verity. But it is instructive that most of his "official" remarks on the positive relationship of art to truth concern the artist's ideal rather than any actual accomplishment. In his renowned preface to *The Nigger of the "Narcissus,"* he wrote that "art itself may be defined as a single-minded attempt to render the highest kind of justice to the visible universe, by bringing to light the truth, manifold and one, underlying its every aspect" (p. xxxvii); in his introductory note to *Under Western Eyes*, he spoke of "my primary conviction that truth alone is the justification of any fiction which makes the least claim to the quality of art" (p. viii); and in his note to the short story volume *Within the Tides*, he commented once more on "that conscientious rendering of truth in thought and fact which has been always my aim" (p. viii).

The degree of confidence that Conrad had in his ability to reveal the underlying truth of the visible world was not, however, very considerable. Doubtless, his most cherished ambition was to shadow forth truth through a meticulous handling of character and event. But even though he had a deep sense of his integrity in transcribing "the truth of [his] own sensations" (*Within the Tides*, p. viii), there is little evidence that he was convinced such truth could be successfully communicated through language. So long as experience derived its meaning only as it was "sensed" by the participant, all attempts to convey experience linguistically involved a perversion of its original meaning. For subjective and objective truth were forever separated, and the former could not be translated into the latter without its vitality—and ultimately, it validity—being forfeited.

Marlow, Conrad's greatest spokesman, has a glimpse into this sad state of affairs when he confesses to his auditors in "Heart of Darkness" his inability to render the felt truth of his contact with Kurtz. He is altogether aware that however much he may dispassionately dissect the ivory trader for his listeners, he can never vitalize the man for them; he can never make them actually *see* the man, as Conrad in the preface to *The Nigger* professed to be his foremost desire. Referring to Kurtz, Marlow despairingly asks his audience: "Do you see him? Do you see the story? Do you see anything? It seems to me I am trying to tell you a dream—making a vain attempt, because no relation of a dream can convey the life-sensation of any given epoch of one's existence—that which makes its truth, its meaning—its subtle and penetrating essence. It is impossible. We live, as we dream—alone. . ." (i.82). If any confession of futility ever sounded definitive, surely it is this one. And it is significant that Conrad's preface to *The Nigger*—an idealistic and optimistic statement of his artistic creed—is dated 1897, while the composition of "Heart of Darkness" follows only two years later. Conrad's first really ambitious fictional undertaking was enough to dispel his treasured illusions about his art. Indeed, Marlow's lament on verbal communication is but an echo of thoughts the author put in a letter of 1898 to W. E. Henley. "Words blow away like mist," he observed, "and like mist they serve only to obscure, to make vague the real shape of one's feelings. . . . Were I to write and talk till Doomsday you would never really know what it all means to me. . .because you never had just the same experience"[2] The lofty belief that art could transcend life by making

[2]18 October 1898, in Baines, *Joseph Conrad,* pp. 218-219.

individual meanings universal was not, obviously, one that the ever-questioning Conrad could long hold.

Melville, as has already been shown, shared Conrad's skepticism of art's ability to transmit truth, and it is no surprise that the word "inscrutable" turns up time after time in both writers' fiction. Although they might similarly have conceived the artist's aim "to evolve the inscrutable" (as Babbalanja chooses to define his intellectual quest [*Mardi*, II.x.36]), they eventually lost faith in their ability to do this, and turned instead to the more modest task of informing their readers of what had, at last, to be regarded as inscrutable. Their most penetrating fiction ends only by revealing deeply rooted problems associated with moral and metaphysical truth; it does not presume to solve them. Or to put it another way, both authors, skeptical of art's power to make private meanings public or to derive absolute meanings from their artistic structurings of experience, deal in their greatest works with perhaps the ultimate human fact: that objective truth is not discernible at all.

With no genuine confidence either in art or life, Melville and Conrad had little left to them but to make of their lack of confidence a "creed" in itself. If all one's beliefs were subject to disappointment, then the sanest — and safest — attitude was one of total skepticism. Not *completely* total, of course, because the stance of skepticism *is* one that can be taken up as a positive (albeit negative) alternative to always-vulnerable faith: if it be a defensive position, it is at least not an escape from one. In *The Confidence-Man,* the bold frontiersman Pitch is able to withstand the specious arguments of the herb doctor as well as he does because — as he replies when asked where he places his confidence — "I have confidence in distrust" (xxi.143). We hardly need note that the necessities of such a wary disposition are strongly supported through the numerous triumphs of the swindler, who is so adept at capitalizing on the natural human urge toward confidence. His carefully calculated evocations of trust for his own insidious purposes expose the dangers of believing in one's fellow-man. We remember how Don

Benito's confidence in the Negro slaves aboard the *San Dominick* leads to their being allowed to move about the vessel freely, and thus to their seizure of it. The Spaniard, undone by his lack of skepticism, is like those exceedingly gullible fish Melville jokes so sadly over in "The Encantadas." Soberly calling them to account for their fatal attraction to man's treacherous bait, he laments: "Poor fish of Rondondo! in your victimised confidence, you are of the number of those who inconsiderately trust, while they do not understand, human nature" (*The Piazza Tales*, iii.198).

The "number" of these too-easily-convinced, of these poor creatures whose fond illusions make them easy game for the countless confidence men of the world, is, as both Melville and Conrad realize, regrettably large. Their vulnerability is defined by their compulsion to believe—and the vast majority of people need desperately, if they are to feel at all secure, to trust in their fellow-man, regardless of how unwarranted that trust may often be. And, poor fish that they are, they must suffer for their insufficiently cultivated distrust. As Conrad tells us in *Nostromo*: "The popular mind is incapable of scepticism; and that incapacity delivers their helpless strength to the wiles of swindlers and to the pitiless enthusiasms of leaders inspired by visions of a high destiny" (III.viii.420). And in *Chance*, where we discover in the great de Barral a character comparable to Melville's archetypal cheat in the breadth of his dishonest operations, the author similarly grieves over man's gullibility. Speaking through his wisely skeptical narrator Marlow, he observes how the financial swindler is "a danger to a moral world inhabited by a credulous multitude not fit to take care of itself" (I.vii.243).

Like Martin Decoud in *Nostromo*, Conrad recognized the need of having "no faith in anything except the truth of his own sensations" (II.vii.229). And although as an ethically orthodox artist he had to disapprove of Decoud's radical unbelief, the structure of his novel undercuts the intellectual legitimacy of all other positions. When, in speaking about his art many years later, Conrad remarked on the "scrupulous fidelity to the truth of my own sensations"

(*Within the Tides*, p. viii), he revealed the foundation of his skepticism as identical to that of his spiritually congenial creation. For having succumbed to what John Henry Newman in his *Apologia* refers to as "the all-corroding, all-dissolving scepticism of the intellect," Conrad was incapable of any faith whatsoever. Like Melville's Pitch, he could have confidence only in distrust; and when he wrote to his friend Edward Garnett: "where is the thing, institution or principle which I do not doubt?!"[3] he clearly set himself apart from such more hopeful contemporaries as Galsworthy, Wells, and Shaw.

Not only was skepticism a practical necessity to Melville and Conrad: it was also the way of wisdom. If nothing in life warranted absolute confidence, then the attitude of continual doubt, of admitting all the possibilities of a thing without committing oneself to any of them, was both the most open-minded and the most enlightened way of "coming to terms" with reality. In *The Secret Agent*, Conrad defines "true wisdom" as that "which is not certain of anything in this world of contradictions" (v.84). And even though in context the absence of this wisdom serves ironically to account for the success of Chief Inspector Heat, the author nevertheless feels it within his rights to criticize the intellectual validity of his conduct. Conrad's censorious manner toward his creation corresponds exactly with the derisive tone implicit in Melville's description of Captain Delano, the wisdom of whose "singularly undistrustful good nature" is called into question. For Melville, knowing all too well the corrupt nature of man, feels obliged to conclude dubiously: "whether in view of what humanity is capable, such a trait implies. . .more than ordinary quickness and accuracy of intellectual perception, may be left to the wise to determine" (*The Piazza Tales*, p. 67). And of course even without the verdict of the wise, we as readers are forced to acknowledge the obtuseness that is a natural by-product of the Captain's deeply ingrained confidence. For his exasperating failure to interpret correctly any of the inci-

[3]*Letters from Joseph Conrad: 1895-1924,* ed. Edward Garnett (Indianapolis, 1928), p. 33.

dents he witnesses demonstrates the perceptual dullness resulting from his irrepressible belief in the integrity of appearances. Lacking the cautious skepticism of a Marlow, he must remain forever uninitiated into the deeper truths of reality.

Having demonstrated how the extensive breakdown of belief in Melville and Conrad leads them to embrace their skepticism as itself a "truth" worthy of propagation in their fiction, we might suggest briefly how this skepticism is manifested in the *method* of their composition. For it is only to be expected that authors so appreciative of the value of distrust in life should be sensitive to its uses in art. Conrad, admonishing his friend John Galsworthy for the lack of skepticism in his work, once paid homage to the doubting perspective by describing it as "the tonic of minds, the tonic of life, the agent of truth, —the way of art and salvation."[4]

If the way toward artistic truth was through the attitude of skepticism, it was, on another level, through the ironic mode of expression. Only by subjecting their narratives to the severe tests of irony did the two writers feel they could communicate their consciousness of the intellectual frailty of all feelings and convictions. Free from all idealistic commitments toward their characters and events, they might better bring out the uncertainties in them which, in the end, constituted their profoundest meaning. The final truth of skepticism could be conveyed artistically through the disinterested examination of its various alternatives, since the ironic method, employed architectonically, presented a universe that gave the lie to all formulas of conduct and belief. Denying the solutions even of art, it could forcefully illustrate life's irresoluble complications.

The "humane" value of such a literary technique may be recognized in its taking us back to the problems of life with increased lucidity, rather than merely enabling us to turn our backs on them. And if we can appreciate the legitimacy of Melville and Conrad's skepticism as an artistic attitude, we are in a sound position to

[4] 11 November 1901, in *Life and Letters*, I, 301.

defend it against the attacks of critics who misconstrue as evasion a manner of presentation that is a fully responsible one, even though its commitment may be only to noncommitment. For example, Irving Howe in his discussion of *The Secret Agent* objects to the fact that while "the qualifications required by irony are present in abundance. . .it is difficult to determine *what* is being qualified, which standard of behavior is being singled out for attack or defense."[5] Such a notion on the unhandy state of affairs prevailing in the novel is, we must admit, accurate enough, and—turning to Melville—it might also account for the interpretive difficulties connected with such works as "Bartleby," "Benito Cereno," *The Confidence-Man,* and *Billy Budd.* All the same, Howe's harsh conclusion that because of *The Secret Agent's* unclear thematic position Conrad's irony must be depreciated as "facile" and "peevish" seems grossly unfair as an evaluation of the author's achievement. It is like finding fault with *Billy Budd* because of Melville's ambivalence toward Captain Vere. What must be realized about both writers is that their apparent refusal to stand firmly in back of any identifiable point of view speaks far more for their integrity and incisiveness as artists than it does for any temperamental incapacity to come to grips with their materials.

Once we accept this idea, the kind of narrative detachment we find in their most notable works can clearly be seen as a strength; for it is calculated to make us especially sensitive to what is taking place, to remove us sufficiently from the individual trees so that we may see the forest in all its terrific density. Our sympathies for the various characters controlled by the irony of their handling, we are forced to become more doubtful about the unstated motives of their behavior. Unable to identify totally with any of the characters, we are eventually made to adopt toward them the same skepticism that went into their creation. The ambiguous elements we discover underlying their actions incline us to view them cautiously, withholding indefinitely any assured belief in them. To say, then, as

[5]*Politics and the Novel* (Cleveland, 1957), p. 96.

does Hugh Kenner about the construction of *Nostromo*, that "Conrad, at bottom, doesn't know what his attitude to his events and characters is, and that is what 'detachment' conceals,"[6] is to disallow unfairly the artistic validity of the skeptical perspective. Detachment, so long as it is used consistently by an author, must be understood as a technique enabling the artist to establish with his reader the relationship most suitable for his purposes. It does not deserve to be passed off as a regrettable lack of decision — or creativity — in the author.

Complementing this method of distancing the reader from the narrative is the employment of a tone that suggests by its irony the deceptiveness of appearances. Through such tonal sarcasm, we are made to suspect not only the integrity of what is presented, but its final cosmic justice as well. When Melville, discoursing on "goodness" in *The Confidence-Man*, speaks of it as "no such rare thing among men," since "the world familiarly know the noun; a common one in every language" (vii.45), the function of his equivocating rhetoric in undercutting what, supposedly, he wishes to propound, is clearly in evidence. For the skeptical author can summon up a belief in goodness only as a verbal entity — as a common noun, not as a common human trait. By immediately withdrawing what he has pretended to offer, he prompts the reader not simply to cancel his original impression (as though nothing, after all, has been asserted), but to move toward the skeptical point of view that inspired such a deliberately misleading statement. The ironic humor plainly discernible in this tongue-in-cheek reflection on "goodness" has also the effect of pulling the reader away from the immediate circumstances provoking the comment, and thus discouraging any too-close involvement in the ever-beguiling narrative. If we study the humor in Conrad's heavily ironic "Outpost of Progress," we will discover a similar comic tone designed to guarantee our detachment toward, and disapproving judgment of, the buffoonish ivory traders, Kayerts and Carlier.

[6]*Gnomon: Essays in Contemporary Literature* (New York, 1958), p. 167.

The most acrid tonal irony of all in Conrad, however, is that which deals not with characters but with circumstances. Disbelieving, like Melville, in a beneficent providence, Conrad was most biting in underscoring the irony of a fate that often seemed far more responsive to the machinations of evil than it did to the entreaties of good. This notion of the mockery of justice probably finds its most caustic expression at the conclusion of "The End of the Tether," where Massy—who has contrived at once to wreck his decaying steamboat so that he might collect his insurance on her, and to lead the old but still admirable Captain Whalley to a pathetic suicide—is shown so gloriously reaping the benefits of his treachery. The author, intentionally underplaying his outrage at Massy's unprincipled success, remarks flatly on the inquiry that pronounces all parties innocent and attributes the shipwreck to an unaccountable drift in the current: "Indeed, it could not have been anything else" (*Youth*, xiv.334).

The whole truth of the wretched affair is lost—just as it also evaporates after the death of Billy Budd, whose noble character is so curiously altered in both the newspaper report and the ballad that make it their subject. In both instances, the reader is forced to wonder about the meaning of it all, and in neither instance does any satisfactory "moral" suggest itself. As a result, the final viewpoint of skepticism emerges as the only valid one. We are left to accept it as we can.

CHAPTER III

NIHILISM:
LOOKING INTO THE DARKNESS

If we are obliged to see Melville and Conrad as profound skeptics, we are also compelled to see them as nihilists. For nihilism in its basic philosophic sense may be defined simply as the radical skepticism toward ever knowing anything. Having already discussed the two writers' disbelief in the possibility of *communicating* truth, we must now show (descending to the "little lower layer") how both authors eventually denied even the possibility of attaining truth. Their recognition of the final futility of constructing meanings for things serves in fact to give their most significant fiction its peculiarly ambiguous qualities.

As serious novelists, both authors were deeply concerned with penetrating to the core of their subjects. But while they may have trusted their probings to reveal man's deeper motives (thus enabling the reader to reach an "informed" position of skepticism about them), they could not convince themselves that their disclosures of man's mixed nature revealed any ultimate grasp of him. It is interesting that Melville's narrator Ishmael, with all his "divine intuitions," does have some inklings about the fundamental mysteries of man, but that he disbelieves in the power of language to do justice to them. After he has analyzed in considerable depth Ahab's "special lunacy," he concludes that while "this is much; yet Ahab's larger, darker, deeper part remains unhinted. But vain to popularise profundities, and all truth is profound" (*M-D*, I.xli.231).

This sentiment is echoed farther on in the novel when he remarks that "whatever is truly wondrous and fearful in man, never yet was put into words or books" (II.cx.246). Indeed, this latter remark may suggest a progression in his disbelief in language, since his skepticism toward communicating the profundities of man's nature here extends to the very notion of their conceptualization. In consequence, when we move beyond Ishmael — and his hopeful intuitions of the truth — to later narrators explicitly concerned with the same problems of apprehension, we discover a point of view virtually synonymous with that of the more secular-minded Conrad.

Unlike Ishmael, the narrators of *Pierre* and *The Confidence-Man* assume no role in their stories outside of making us particularly aware of their sensibilities in the telling. Not included in the dramatis personae, they more naturally appear to speak directly for the author, and we commit no serious critical error in referring to the two of them as Melville himself. Here is the Melville who has ceased to believe in the art of telling the truth, and his doubtful sentiments lead us directly to that cognitive darkness so intensely realized by the likewise disenchanted Conrad. In *Pierre*, the author first observes the mysterious nature of man by relating it to his unfathomable Creator. He tells us of his hero's sudden recognition that "human life doth truly come from that, which all men are agreed to call by the name of *God*; and that it partakes of the unravellable inscrutableness of God" (VII.viii.199). Or, to put it in a somewhat more logical fashion, so long as man's reason is befuddled by the operations of the universe, it can never pretend to detect absolute meaning in the human situation. All quests to discover the truth of man are doomed from the start, for man's soul is infinite and his capacity for comprehension finite. Melville's classic statement on the insurmountable barriers of human perception comes in *Pierre*, when he is moved to reflect: "Deep, deep, and still deep and deeper must we go, if we would find out the heart of man; descending into which is as descending a spiral stair in a shaft, without any end, and where that endlessness is only concealed by the spiralness of the stair, and the blackness of the shaft"

(XXI.ii.402). Here is Melville's "heart of darkness," and, like Conrad's, nothing can illuminate it.

In *The Confidence-Man*, where the author has passed beyond the despairing viewpoint so noticeable in *Pierre*, he is at least able to affirm the artistic usefulness of a frank confession of man's unknowability. For if an author admits that "human nature. . .is past finding out, [he] thereby evinces a better appreciation of it than he who, by always representing it in a clear light, leaves it to be inferred that he clearly knows all about it" (xiv.91). We recall Conrad's writing to Galsworthy that skepticism was the way of art, and in this quotation we may recognize something of the same attitude. Here once again the two authors' metaphysical stance can be seen as influencing their working aesthetic. This aesthetic may seem at first anti art in its refusal to "formalize" its subjects, but in its truthful portrayal of man's incomprehensible self it is actually representative of the most authentic art of all. It honestly looks into mysteries: it does not betray them through any artfully calculated resolution.

Even in Conrad's *Nigger of the "Narcissus"*—which focuses upon certain recognizable human types—the author hints at his awareness that human nature is past finding out by telling us at one point that the stars glittering above the sea are "as inscrutable as the souls of men" (ii.29). And while Conrad might scrutinize relentlessly the enigma of James Wait and the moral complexities of the crew's fascination with him, his assessment of the facts is given through a rhetoric better suited to demonstrating the essential ambiguities of the situation than to revealing any supposed truths about the state of man's soul. For what could be surmised about the crew's response to the dying Wait only raised other, ultimate questions, the answers to which could not be surmised at all. Marlow's quest for Kurtz follows a similar pattern, for while Marlow may be conscious of the egoistic foundation for the ivory trader's inflated idealism, the soul of Kurtz remains hopelessly vague to him. As he says of the awesome egomaniac: "His was an impenetrable darkness. I looked at him as you peer down at a man who is lying at the bottom of a precipice where the sun never shines" (*Youth*, iii.149). Marlow's voyage may, metaphorically, take him directly to the heart of man, but this heart is yet too dark to be made out clearly, and so Marlow can never understand the full meaning of "the horror," which apparently we are to see as signifying Kurtz's most profound vision of human life. The Marlow of *Lord Jim* discovers himself in the same predicament, for though Jim may be understood as "one of us," the narrator still feels obliged to regard him as impenetrable. He cannot believe in the possibility of ever deriving the essential truth about him—either by watching him or listening to him. Early in the novel Marlow wonderingly describes one of Jim's conversations with him by observing the youth's problematic manner of expression: "He talked soberly, with a sort of composed unreserve, and with a quiet bearing that might have been the outcome of manly self-control, of impudence, of callousness, of a colossal unconsciousness, of a gigantic deception. Who can tell!" (vii.78). As Bartleby must remain unknown to the narrator who makes so many attempts to penetrate him, as Benito Cereno must always be incomprehensible to Captain Delano, so Jim's true nature must continue to puzzle the constantly delving Marlow. For no matter how intelligent a person's inferences about the innermost reality of another may be, these inferences can never achieve the status of truth, which must stay forever obscure and out of view.

If it is impossible to unravel the truth of man by identifying with another's spiritual crisis (or, indeed, by turning one's gaze inward—and Conrad once wrote that "one's own personality is only a ridiculous and aimless masquerade of something hopelessly unknown"[1]), it is no less impossible to fathom the world outside man. Both Melville and Conrad had the same idea of cosmic inscrutability, and were inclined to feel resentment toward a world hostile to all of man's attempts to penetrate it. Alien to man, the natural

---

[1] 23 March 1896, in *Letters*, ed. Garnett, p. 46.

universe appeared a mercilessly indifferent master over him as well. It could ruthlessly set up the conditions for Kurtz's ethical deterioration or, if we see the white whale as its symbol, it could plunge a helpless crew to its drowning depths. Eternally resisting all of man's endeavors at comprehension, it seemed to strike back at all those who dared to strike through it.

Ahab, who needs desperately to assume a significance in the workings of nature, proclaims that "all visible objects. . .are but as pasteboard masks," and courageously adds that "if man will strike, strike through the masks!" (*M-D*, I.xxxvi.204), but toward the end of his fatal search he is led to remark that "the dead, blind wall butts all inquiring heads at last" (II.cxxv.300). By dramatizing Ahab's futile quest for the whale, Melville indirectly reveals his own conception of the impenetrable universe—one which, to borrow a phrase from Marlow, is "too dark altogether." Like Ahab, Ishmael reveals a sense of nature's imperviousness in conceding the final superficiality of all his descriptions of the whale. He, too, would like to descend to the "little lower layer" but is forced to acknowledge: "Dissect him [the whale] how I may, then, I but go skin deep; I know him not, and never will" (II.1xxxvi.123). Regardless of how many facts Ishamel, or anyone else, might assemble in the hope of discovering the essence of a thing, that thing is destined to remain partly enshrouded in darkness—for, in terms of human perception, its obscurity is an intrinsic part of its nature. Man can never bridge the gap between the sum of its known facts and its essential meaning. By learning all he can about it, he is only made more aware of its fathomlessness.

"Benito Cereno" and *Lord Jim* may each be seen as dealing specifically with this insoluble problem of human comprehension. In Melville's tale, the final meaning of Don Benito's confrontation with the Negro remains hidden, despite all the narrative's scrupulous attempts to shadow it forth. After the credulous Captain Delano has finally been undeceived about the situation on board the *San Dominick* and we are presented with a generous sampling of the court depositions on the wretched affair, we are still left with

Captain Delano at a distant remove from the ultimate human meaning contained in the Spaniard's torturous experience. The narrative may put us into closer contact with man's nature by faithfully rendering its darkest manifestations, but because it depicts only the outward spectacle of human experience, it can never unveil its "soul," that which might make its final import lucid.

In a like manner, the facts that emerge in *Lord Jim* through the official inquiry into Jim's case are pronounced insufficient in yielding the truth about Jim. The meaning of the youth's regrettable failure to pass the ethical test provided by the precarious situation on board the *Patna* can never be derived through public examination. We are told how the court audience is eager to understand the facts of the situation, but the futility of their hopes is rudely exposed by the remark: "They wanted facts. Facts! They demanded facts from him, as if facts could explain anything!" (iv.29). As in the court depositions in "Benito Cereno," any facts that may come to light are capable of explaining only the "superficial how" of the matter and not the "fundamental why" (*LJ*, vi.56). Even Jim, who in his need to understand—and also forgive himself for—an act that in itself he is obliged to recognize as culpable, fares no better in his conscientiously determined quest for the truth. In addressing the court, "He wanted to go on talking for truth's sake. . .[and] his mind positively flew round and round the serried circle of facts"; but answering question after question and yet coming no closer to making manifest the crucial meaning of his experience, he feels tempted at one point to exclaim, "What's the good of this! what's the good!" (iv.31-32). The fundamental meaning embedded in his moral failing must forever resist both his attempts and those of others to root it out. Marlow reminds us some pages later of the large turnout at Jim's trial and interprets the audience's attraction to the case by speaking of their "expectation of some essential disclosure as to the strength, the power, the horror, of human emotions." But, as he reflects, "the examination of the only man able and willing to face it [the disclosure] was beating futilely round the well-known fact, and the play of questions upon it was as instructive as the tapping with a hammer on an iron box, were the object to find out what's inside" (vi.56).

Such a metaphor of cognitive futility parallels that of Babbalanja in *Mardi* (or, to be exact, of Bardianna, Babbalanja's favorite wise man, whose words he is so fond of quoting): "'Fellowmen; the ocean we would sound is unfathomable; and however much we add to our line, when it is out, we feel not the bottom' " (II.1xxi.301). The inaccessibility of truth degrades the acquisition of facts to a mere intellectual pastime. For basically, we must deal either with a strongbox without a key or with an ocean without a bottom: in the one instance we cannot penetrate inward, in the other we cannot reach far enough downward. Similarly, the images of the heart of darkness and the pasteboard mask serve to negate the possibility of ever perceiving inmost truth. Here the end of our symbolic voyage for meaning leaves us either in front of a heart whose features we have not the light to illumine, or before a mask that has mysteriously hardened to a "dead, blind wall," which resistantly butts all heads bold enough to try to pierce it.

In *Pierre*, Melville is most explicit of all about the hopelessness of attaining truth. After Pierre's illusions about his father's grandiose virtue are dispelled, the hero determines that: "Henceforth I will know nothing but Truth; glad Truth, or sad Truth; I will know what *is*. . ." (III.vi.90). Seeing how his immense filial adoration has been without substance, he will now abandon his unquestioned faith and tear the veils off all his idols so he may espy whatever lurks behind them. But much later, when he vainly attempts to set down in his book the dark, underlying realities of life, he is made to see "the everlasting elusiveness of Truth" (XXV.iii.472).

The Marlow of *Lord Jim* expresses precisely the same viewpoint when, in a sudden rhetorical flourish, he reflects that "absolute Truth. . .floats elusive, obscure, half submerged, in the silent still waters of mystery" (xx.216). Finally, all attempts at establishing meaning had to be recognized as pretense, for the only reality man could know was fated to be illusory. Conrad put forth this nihilistic regard for human existence most emphatically in a letter to Edward Garnett, in which he sadly remarked:

> All is illusion — the words written, the mind at which they are aimed, the truth they are intended to express, the hands that will hold the paper, the eyes that will glance at the lines. Every image floats vaguely in a sea of doubt — and the doubt itself is lost in an unexplored universe of incertitudes.[2]

The absolute doubt of skepticism becomes itself conjectural when placed against the measureless background of cosmic enigma. We are reminded here of the radically isolated Decoud, for whom "the affectations of irony and skepticism have no place." Burdened with the weight of unrelieved solitude and having lost "the sustaining illusion of an independent existence," he beholds the world as "a succession of incomprehensible images" (*Nostromo*, III.x.497-498).

Since in the end nothing definitive can ever be known, it follows that there can be no fixed standards for evaluating the morality of human behavior. In their most searching works, Melville and Conrad evidence a sad awareness of this situation, and however repellent they may find it are obliged to admit its logic. Generally speaking, Melville's "quest novels" and Conrad's "test novels" each in their own way disclose the same ambiguities about the moral universe. The ultimately undefinable nature of personalities and events is seen as precluding the possibility of any absolutely sanctioned code of ethics. Thus all ideas of good and evil had to be recognized as tenuous, essentially unrelated to man's eternal condition.

It is interesting that even Marlow, Conrad's greatest moralist, is (at least before *Chance*) skeptical about the validity of the prescribed moral code to which he adheres so earnestly. His unsettling experiences with Kurtz and Jim serve alike to weaken the strength of his honorable convictions. On looking back at his somewhat exaggerated interest in Jim's case, he remarks to his auditors that clearly he must have hoped that his close scrutiny of the situation

[2]16 September 1899, in *Letters*, p. 155.

would "lay the ghost" of his plaguing doubt in "the sovereign power enthroned in a fixed standard of conduct." His mournful conclusion is simply that he had "hoped for the impossible" (*LJ*, v.50). He realizes that he can never condemn the erring Jim, for he can never fully believe in the controlling nature of the principles that he would like to apply categorically—and confidently—to Jim's conduct.

If Marlow can yet stop short of utter nihilism, it is because he has what he refers to in "Heart of Darkness" as a "deliberate belief" (*Youth*, ii.97), a conviction in the absolute *value* of such traits as courage, restraint, duty, and fidelity. Turning to Melville's *Pierre*, we may witness how once the hero bids farewell to his unsubstantiated faith, he advances steadily toward ethical nihilism. Having lost so much of his piety, he dares consider whether "Life be a cheating dream, and virtue as unmeaning and unsequelled with any blessing as the midnight mirth of wine" (VII.v.189). Such unorthodox speculation, Melville recognizes, is dangerous; and standing between his hero and the reader, he later issues the following warning (a warning that Conrad would certainly have understood):

> In those Hyperborean regions, to which enthusiastic Truth, and Earnestness, and Independence, will invariably lead a mind fitted by nature for profound and fearless thought, all objects are seen in a dubious, uncertain, and refracting light. Viewed through that rarefied atmosphere the most immemorially admitted maxims of men begin to slide and fluctuate, and finally become wholly inverted. . . .
>
> But the example of many minds forever lost, like undiscoverable Arctic explorers, amid those treacherous regions, warns us entirely away from them; and we learn that it is not for man to follow the trail of truth too far, since by so doing he entirely loses the directing compass of his mind; for arrived at the Pole, to whose barrenness only it points, there, the needle indifferently respects all points of the horizon alike. (IX.i.231)

Pierre, unfortunately, is too determined a soul to heed such a warning, and eventually we find him propounding to Isabel the illusoriness of moral categories: "Look: a nothing is the substance, it casts one shadow one way, and another the other way; and these two shadows cast from one nothing; these, seems to me, are Virtue and Vice" (XIX.ii.382). He must consequently regard the traditional notions of good and evil as utterly beside the point, being man-made and having no perceptible relationship to the world outside man. This discovery constitutes his "horror" and it is not unlike that of Kurtz, whose vision of the all-encompassing darkness of existence makes him terrifyingly aware of man's perilous freedom.

Both Melville and Conrad recognized that as long as the universe remained an infinite vacancy to man, no set of moral principles could have any objective foundation. Thus human life was "absurd": the morality of man had nothing whatever to do with a universe that itself could be seen only as amoral. Indeed, the word "absurd," like the word "inscrutable," turns up with considerable frequency in the writings of the two authors. Further, if no ideals could be categorically justified, all of them, even the noblest, were "unreal" — mere products of the imagination. A Confidence Man might practice his swindling techniques on board a ship ironically named the *Fidèle* and hope for as much eternal reward as a saint. For the world could only be seen as looking on indifferently at man's actions. As Conrad once noted: "The ethical view of the universe involves us at last in so many cruel and absurd contradictions, where the last vestiges of faith, hope, and charity, and even of reason itself, seem ready to perish, that I have come to suspect that the aim of creation cannot be ethical at all" (*A Personal Record*, v.92). And even at a time when Conrad was completing his sentimental and philosophically shallow *The Arrow of Gold*, he could write to his friend Garnett:

> Bitterness is the very condition of human existence, and mankind generally is neither guilty nor innocent. It simply is. . . . Intelligence itself [is] a thing of no great account except for us to torment ourselves with. For directly you begin to use it the questions of right and wrong arise and these are things of the air with no connection whatever with the fundamental realities of life.[3]

[3] 16 May 1918, in *Letters*, p. 258.

Melville, whose own anti-intellectualism had a similarly intellectual source, shared with Conrad this basically nihilistic stance toward morality. Having a greater consciousness of heredity as a determiner of man's behavior, however, he complemented his disenchanted nihilism with a keen sense of moral determinism. Since man's ethical life was foreordained by his natural endowment, society's moral code—made ultimately irrelevant by its disconnection with the natural universe—was also immediately irrelevant because its assumption that man had a choice over his conduct falsified his nature. We find this idea of ethical fatalism first expressed in *Mardi*, then re-expressed in *Redburn, White Jacket,* and *Billy Budd*, where it is embodied—always negatively—in the persons of Jackson, Bland, and Claggart.

In *Mardi*, Babbalanja is driven to reflect that men "are governed by their very natures" and that, therefore, "it is easier for some men to be saints, than for others not to be sinners" (II.xxxix.156). Jackson in *Redburn* is surely one of these natural sinners, for we are told that he is "spontaneously an atheist and an infidel." He seems to have no moral alternative open to him, for he is described as "a Cain afloat; branded on his yellow brow with some inscrutable curse" (xxii.134). In *White Jacket*, we learn that the villainous master-at-arms, Bland, is "an organic and irreclaimable scoundrel, who did wicked deeds as the cattle browse the herbage, because wicked deeds seemed the legitimate operation of his whole infernal organisation" (xliv.234). Melville's most memorable figure of predestined evil is, of course, Claggart, and by this time the author has settled upon a particularly fitting appellation for the type. Adopting Plato's definition of "Natural Depravity," he illustrates its appropriateness to an even more villainous master-at-arms than the unscrupulous Bland. Claggart, he informs us, harbors within him "the mania of an evil nature, not engendered by vicious training or corrupting books or licentious living, but born with him and innate, in short, 'a depravity according to nature' " (*BB*, x.46). In the chapter directly following, we are given another description of Claggart, which, by recognizing him as a slave to his destiny, virtually exonerates him from all future blame. Melville writes of the master-at-arms as having "no power to annul the elemental evil in himself," and as at once "apprehending the good, but powerless to be it"—an unrectifiable situation which forces him to "act out to the end [his nature's] allotted part" (xi.49). Seen in this light, the unself-conscious virtue of a Budd is no more worthy of praise than the unchosen villainy of a Claggart is deserving of condemnation. In the end, Melville's probings of man and the universe belied not just the soundness, but in a sense even the "fairness," of conventional moral categories.

Forced to admit the invalidity of every system of morality and metaphysics, Melville and Conrad had little in which to take comfort. The transcendental idealism and philosophic optimism common in both Europe and America during the nineteenth century could not but appear to them vain and insubstantial. Indeed, their fictional personages—from Taji to Billy Budd and from the crew of the *Narcissus* to Heyst—functioned in one way or other to rebut dramatically all current proofs of the positive nature of human life. Objectively considered, only the position of nihilism—of general unbelief—could be supported convincingly. Permanently alienated from cosmic truth, man was destined to cope everlastingly with appearances. Any knowledge he might acquire about his condition was relative and therefore unable to provide him with reliable standards of conduct. All the speculations on morality, philosophy, and religion found in the greatest fiction of Melville and Conrad may be interpreted as serving the similar purpose of crystallizing the two authors' discouraged agnosticism—a stance that, as we have seen, ultimately fuses with nihilism.

Going hand in hand with this nihilism is an attitude of deep pessimism. In his critical biography on Conrad, Jocelyn Baines speaks of *Nostromo* as "an intensely pessimistic book. . .perhaps the most impressive monument to futility ever created,"[4] and we may note this same underlying gloom not only in other key works

[4]*Joseph Conrad*, p. 310.

by Conrad, but also in such fictional pieces of Melville's as *Pierre,* "Bartleby," and *The Confidence-Man.* The first two works end with suicides made to seem about as fruitful as anything preceding them; the third tale ends, ironically, as it began—on April Fools' Day, a most pointed suggestion on the author's part of the "fiendish and appalling joke" that Marlow in *Lord Jim* (see x.121) judged as characterizing man's abiding condition.

Because neither author could hope that man's lot on earth would improve, both had to regard negatively all proposed solutions for human ills. As Conrad at his bleakest wrote to Cunninghame Graham: "In a dispassionate view the ardour for reform, improvement, for virtue, for knowledge and even for beauty is only a vain sticking up for appearances, as though one were anxious about the cut of one's clothes in a community of blind men."[5] And in another letter to Graham written about the same time, Conrad's sense of life's futility finds expression in words that could not possibly be more explicit as a pronouncement of his far-reaching nihilism: "There is no morality, no knowledge and no hope; there is only the consciousness of ourselves which drives us about a world that, whether seen in a convex or a concave mirror, is always but a vain and floating appearance."[6] It is certainly no coincidence that in the year these letters were written, Conrad was also at work on "Heart of Darkness," his other "impressive monument to futility." We can appreciate the author's essential identity with his most famous narrator when Marlow is made to remark after the death of Kurtz: "Droll thing life is—that mysterious arrangement of merciless logic for a futile purpose" (*Youth,* iii.150). It would seem in fact that it is Kurtz's own recognition of the absurdity of his fate, a fate making all acts permissible, that constitutes the meaning of his final cry: "The horror! The horror!"

Only in *Pierre* can we see Melville explicitly acknowledging the idea of a senseless universe, although as we have already implied, "Bartleby" and *The Confidence-Man* are vividly recognizable

[5]14 January 1898, in *Life and Letters,* I, 222.
[6]31 January 1898, in *Life and Letters,* I, 226.

as artistic statements of the author's nihilism. There is, however, a reflection in a letter of Melville's — written, interestingly enough, two decades after he had abdicated his role as novelist — that would seem to identify his worldly perspective closely with Conrad's: "Life is so short, and so ridiculous and irrational. . .that one knows not what to make of it, unless — well, finish the sentence for yourself."[7] Even at this later, and more conservative, period of the author's existence, we can detect his contemplating (though now not quite daring to articulate) the possibility of life's having no reasonable plan or purpose. In both Melville and Conrad we see how speculating without bias or preconception on the human enterprise can lead to the sorrowful conclusion that no arguments ever advanced to explain life's object have any real substance. The only position defensible in the face of life's endless contradictions and uncertainties was nihilism; and if the two authors had to respect its validity, they hardly rejoiced in its being the sole "answer" to their questionings. For such a conclusion robbed them of all faith and left them forlorn. It is surely noteworthy that Tony Tanner, in discussing the pessimism of *Lord Jim*, sees fit to bring in Melville as another creative mind whose fiction tended toward despair: "It seems to me that Conrad reached that last stage of pessimism which very few other writers — Melville is one — have experienced. The stage at which the greatest fear is not that the meaning of life might be evil but that there might be absolutely no meaning at all to be found."[8]

The nihilistic vision of Melville and Conrad may be seen as defining the very real ambiguity in their writings as itself a "theme" or "subject." Though the two authors may have been bewildered by life's complexities, they did not turn away from them in their fiction, and the outcome is that their books are themselves

    [7]To John C. Hoadley, 31 March 1877, in *The Letters of Herman Melville,* ed. Merrell R. Davis and William H. Gilman (New Haven, Conn., 1960), p. 260.
    [8]"Butterflies and Beetles — Conrad's Two Truths," *Chicago Review,* XVI (1963), 136.

often bewildering. Fascinated with all the discrepancies of existence and wishing to portray them honestly in their fiction, they endeavored to adapt the form of art to the formless mysteries of life. If their most ambitious works are in the end thematically irresoluble, it is because their subjects are *conceived* as essentially enigmatic; thus to clarify them would be only to falsify them.

E. M. Forster's famous complaint about Conrad's obscurity (seconded later by F. R. Leavis) seems from this standpoint far off target. Forster accused Conrad of being "misty in the middle as well as at the edges" and suspected that "the secret casket of his genius contain[ed] a vapour rather than a jewel,"[9] but assuredly as long as Conrad—or, for that matter, any author—managed to throw some light upon the mist before him, he was accomplishing as much as he might. The way in which the narrator proper of "Heart of Darkness" speaks of Marlow's tale-telling elucidates the modest rationale behind Conrad's own consciously "blurred" narrative perspective. "The yarns of seamen," he tells us, "have a direct simplicity, the whole meaning of which lies within the shell of a cracked nut. But Marlow was not typical. . .and to him the meaning of an episode was not inside like a kernel but outside, enveloping the tale which brought it out only as a glow brings out a haze. . ." (*Youth,* i.48). To Marlow, as to Conrad, the meaning of an experience is to be discovered, paradoxically, in the very fogginess emergent through the truthful rendering of it: in the tale's obscurity might be detected the artist's mode of seeing. Though such reasoning may appear to illustrate Yvor Winters' "imitational fallacy" with a vengeance, the mistiness in the best works of Melville and Conrad does warrant appreciation as an artistically expressed "vision" of things. It is not, for instance, simply because Conrad is nebulous about Kurtz and Jim, or because Melville remains vague about Bartleby and the Confidence Man, that we can never be quite certain we understand these characters. If the darkness about them is never fully dispelled, it is because although both

[9]*Abinger Harvest* (New York, 1936), p. 138.

writers could visualize such personages sharply and handle them with great authenticity, they could never be confident of their ability to enter imaginatively into their peculiar psyches. Thus only a limited narrative viewpoint could maintain any integrity toward both the perceived and the perceiver.

No one has more strongly expressed the cryptic nature of Conrad's art than Morton Zabel, who in his introduction to *Lord Jim* observes of the book: "It dramatizes an ambiguity; its method and language are ambiguous; it insists on the 'enigma' of its theme and hero; its final effect and import are elusive."[10] In concluding inconclusively, the book faithfully reflects the imagination that created it — an imagination that "insisted" on its inability to clear away the eternal mists of life. In Melville, this same commitment toward the "everlasting elusiveness of truth" is apparent in the curiously "expedient" endings to such works as *Pierre*, "Bartleby," "Benito Cereno," *The Confidence-Man*, and *Billy Budd*. What could be seen and what could be definitively interpreted were two vastly different things. As Marlow notes in *Lord Jim*, "There was always a doubt of [Jim's] courage." And though Marlow may endeavor time after time to ascertain whether the youth's conduct after the *Patna* incident "amounted to shirking his ghost or to facing him out," he is at last forced to confess the ultimate futility of his ruminations by pointing out that "as with the complexion of all our actions, the shade of difference was so delicate that it was impossible to say. It might have been flight and it might have been a mode of combat" (xix.197).

In like fashion, Melville in his many revisions of *Billy Budd* revealed himself at a loss to interpret finally the intrepidity, or inflexibility, symbolized by Captain Vere's decision to execute Budd. What all this suggests is that the dispassionate search for fundamental truth leads only to the "disclosure" of its countless ambiguities. Ironically, it is in our very understanding that nothing is ever ultimately revealed that we may best derive the meaning of

---

[10]"Introduction" to *Lord Jim* (Boston, 1958), p.xxxiii.

Ishmael's "image of the ungraspable phantom of life," which he declares as itself "the key to it all" (*M-D*, I.i.4). The self is unknowable and to try, like Narcissus, to grasp it by plunging into its boundless waters, is to relinquish forever what little contact can be had with it. Both Melville and Conrad were aware of man's need to accept the innate limits of his perception, for to engage himself recklessly with life's phantoms might eventuate in destroying his capacities for perception altogether.

The most that could be hoped for in terms of man's restricted consciousness was to attend to life's obscurities in so dedicated a manner that the exact point at which they defied further scrutiny could be better located. Such a measured investigation of human events is descriptive of Melville's and Conrad's most notable works. Both writers attempt, by journeying relentlessly toward the vital center of their subjects, to show precisely where the heart becomes too dark for further inspection. In *Pierre*, for example, Melville chooses to close one of his discussions by confessing himself incapable of any more advancing: "But here we draw a veil," he tells us. "Some nameless struggles of the soul cannot be painted, and some woes will not be told. Let the ambiguous procession of events reveal their own ambiguousness" (X.iii.253). In consequence of such authorial surrender, what we as readers are made to apprehend is something at once profound and mysterious. It is not simply that we are given nothing to see, for to glimpse the heart's darkness is surely a significant sight. But our final awareness remains insufficient to sketch in the reality we seek. We are left in the position of Marlow, whose contact with Kurtz in the Congo may be recognized as "the culminating point of my experience," but does not, all the same, succeed in assuring him that he has at last had the veils of life removed for him. As he soberly notes: "It seemed somehow to throw a kind of light on everything about me — and into my thoughts. It was sombre enough, too — and pitiful — not extraordinary in any way — not very clear either. No, not very clear. And yet it seemed to throw a kind of light" (*Youth*, i.51). Undoubtedly, whatever wisdom the narrator has gained is of the most hesitant variety, and we, too, are obliged to confess our inability to draw any ultimate conclusions from a narrative specifically defined in the story itself as "inconclusive" (see i.51).

Also self-consciously inconclusive is *The Confidence-Man*, where Melville chooses to "end" his cryptic narrative with the line: "Something further may follow of this Masquerade." In the endeavor to make us comprehend what is at last beyond our power to comprehend, the author determines to arouse confusion about the final meaning of the different episodes, and, through a host of techniques, maintain that confusion until the ambiguity itself is perceived as constituting the inmost meaning of the various scenes. We are eventually forced to accept the novel's radically limited narrative perspective as symbolizing our own limited capacity to "see" what goes on around us. Only in becoming more sensible of our incapability of judging the world that is dramatized for us can we learn the lesson of ambiguity it is Melville's express purpose to inculcate.

Melville's artistically coherent achievement of ambiguity in *The Confidence-Man* is also recognizable in the masterly construction of "Benito Cereno." At least two critics have shown themselves aware of the tale's curious success in its implicit admission of failure, and both of their remarks may be quoted here. To Max Putzel:

> He [Melville] is revising what Delano himself had experienced, elucidating what baffled Delano, and going on to shadow forth a higher, more lucid reality, which baffles himself. What establishes the greatness of the work is that Melville sees a universe like Shakespeare's or Sophocles', where seeming and being interreflect in an endless series, where suggestive ambiguities are as close as man can come to truth, and where the wisest man must admit he sees only a little more than the fool.[11]

And to Barry Phillips:

> The critics of *Benito Cereno* fail for the same reason Amasa Delano fails. They place the problems of the story in the realm of

[11]"The Source and the Symbols of Melville's *Benito Cereno*," in *A "Benito Cereno" Handbook*, ed. Seymour L. Gross (Belmont, Calif., 1965), p. 167.

concepts when all the concepts of the story point to the primary problem of perception. They assign absolute values when the only values are relative. They find objective meaning in experiences whose main significance is the ambiguous, multi-leveled, mysterious nature of experience, and the subjective, albeit emphatically empirical, nature of the only real meaning. . . . [12]

In the most penetrating works of Melville and Conrad, we are thus confronted with qualities of obscurity forever striving to gain legitimate thematic status. That they can in fact attain the level of subjective truth so often is a good index of their creators' artistic skill. And that this final ambiguity can be so convincing a "solution" provides dramatic validation of the logic behind the two authors' nihilistic vision.

[12] " 'The Good Captain': Amasa Delano, American Idealist," in *A "Benito Cereno" Handbook*, p. 111.

CHAPTER IV

THE TECHNIQUES OF INSCRUTABILITY

Having shown how the nihilism of Melville and Conrad leads not just to thematic ambiguity but to ambiguity as theme, we might examine the chief artistic vehicles for this "message" of obscurity. Since the loyalty of both authors to their deepest vision made them critical of conventional literary artifices, they adopted new techniques or meaningfully revised established ones. In their fiction, the connotations of traditional symbols are purposefully inverted; endings are left "open," leaving us in doubt about the issues we had expected to be resolved; rhetoric is often employed not to mitigate our confusion but to justify it — or, in fact, add to it; and, lastly, the omniscient viewpoint is abandoned for a far more restricted one, which tends to minimize our sense of the tale's objective reality.

To say, first of all, that the import of both Melville's and Conrad's symbolism is at times uncertain is not itself to say anything noteworthy. For all symbols, by their very suggestiveness, tend to elude definition. Establishing a significant link between the two writers' symbolic methods, therefore, requires more than a demonstration of how both employed symbols of unruly and expansive meanings. Rather, what is required is an examination of the authors' most conscious handling of those materials traditionally lending themselves to a particular symbolic significance. Or, to put it more clearly perhaps, we must be able to recognize in their symbol-making a thoughtful attempt to disappoint the conventional expectations of what a thing stands for. In Eliot's *Waste Land*, April as the year's "cruelest month" is undoubtedly an April whose traditional connotations have been subverted to convey a sharply antithetical point of view. Forced by the poetic context to re-evaluate the month's spiritual meaning, we must acknowledge that Eliot's April is a creation peculiarly his own and thus understandable only through a careful scrutiny of his poem. In like manner, all symbols calculated to evoke an unprecedented response from the reader warrant appreciation as essentially "private"; as such, they may tell us something of interest about the author's perception. It can, I think, be demonstrated that Melville and Conrad's most deliberate treatment of symbols indicates a similar concern with throwing popularly accepted outlooks into doubt, by way of supporting their notion of reality as objectively undeterminable.

This is not the place for a full-scale consideration of the two writers' symbolism, but a brief look at how each suspected the virtuous characteristics associated with all that was "white" may serve to indicate one way that they contrived to convey a point of view directly challenging the one most broadly held. For in both authors the symbolic signification of white is often not positive at all, but rather of the most dubious moral standing.

The chapter "The Whiteness of the Whale" in *Moby-Dick* constitutes Melville's most famous statement of the color's ambiguity — though, as Charles Feidelson has pointed out in his *Symbolism and American Literature*, Melville handles whiteness with similar symbolic intent in *Mardi* and *White Jacket*.[1] Ishmael's extensive discussion of the color's divine and devilish aspects provides us, however, with the best index of the author's meaningful ambivalence toward it. For, placing the color in a wide variety of contexts, he has his narrator consider the frightening possibility that white may reflect a world without significance or value. Ishmael may at first remind us of several agreeable associations that white has with things both secular and sacred, but he then goes on to declare

[1]Chicago, 1953. See pp. 170, 181, 322-323.

his terror at "an elusive something [that lurks] in the innermost idea of the hue" (*M-D*, I.xlii.235). His contemplation of such repugnant or distasteful qualities as the ferocity of the white bear and the white shark, the fearsomeness of the albino man, and the ghastly pallor of the dead and of ghosts rising out of a white fog, suggests to him that whiteness is "at once the most meaning symbol of spiritual things, nay, the very veil of the Christian's Deity; and yet. . .[also] the intensifying agent in things the most appalling to mankind" (I.xlii.243). Ultimately, Ishmael is led to regard white as the underlying hue of the whole world—as the "colourless, all-colour" that is, mysteriously, the basic law of the universe. It is this perception that leaves him awed at the color's ambiguities and casts into profound doubt his faith in a purposeful, benevolent cosmos. The uncertain and endlessly shifting qualities of whiteness are eventually attached to the white whale, and Moby Dick is thus himself viewed as a natural mystery, reflective of the unfathomable universe that has unaccountably produced him. As such, he cannot be written down either as good or evil, because he is emblematic of the very principle of cosmic inscrutability. Essentially ambiguous, he may be seen as a particularly apt symbol for Melville's nihilistic conception of the natural world. Infinitely suggestive of meanings, he is at the same time everlastingly elusive. The apparently innocent and benign garb of whiteness that is his outer covering—and which is all man can see of him—functions in revealing the deceptiveness of appearances in a world where external facts have no ascertainable relationship to internal reality.

In Conrad, too, white is often seen as a color that, because of the contradictory things to which it affixes itself, belies all clear-cut notions of it. It is a hue whose significations are fluid and forever changing and that, therefore, had better not be "read" indiscriminately. Just as Conrad repeatedly reveals skepticism at man's supposed virtues, so does he suspect the moral purity of all that shares this most "untainted" of hues. For the color of a thing is only its outward aspect and Conrad harbored a general distrust in appearances. This is not to say that he employed whiteness throughout his literary career in any methodically anti-conventional way, for in some works, such as *Victory*, his light-dark symbolism is traditional enough. But in a number of his major fictions, white, or lightness in general, takes on symbolic dimensions that prompt us to regard it as, indeed, altogether "gray" in its final import. The narrator of *The Nigger of the "Narcissus,"* for instance, seems unsure about the relative moral value assignable to light—and to dark, its complement; and the narrator of *Under Western Eyes* appears expressly desirous of illustrating the negative possibilities of whiteness when at one point he remarks of the repulsive Château Borel: "The very light, pouring through a large window at the end [of the corridor], seemed dusty; and a solitary speck reposing on the balustrade of white marble. . .asserted itself extremely, black and glossy in all that crude whiteness" (III.ii.226).

It is in "Heart of Darkness," however, that we may best recognize the author's use of white to demonstrate systematically the ambiguity or downright fraudulence of external reality. Here the misleading aspects of what is observed are frequently mirrored in a schematic reversal of the symbolic values conventionally attached to light and dark. Brussels, we are told, reminds the narrator of a "whited sepulchre" (*Youth*, i.55); the white men so mercilessly grubbing for their percentages in the ivory trade have the blackest of souls (while, on the other hand, the blacks whom they domineer impress us as the most innocent of victims); and the accountant's refreshingly "civilized" and dazzling white costume stands in direct opposition to his brutal unconcern with the natives suffering and dying everywhere about him. Most notable of all, the light that surrounds the Intended at the tale's close is defined not as the light of truth but of faithful, loving illusions; while her visitor Marlow, who brings with him the terrible facts of Kurtz's moral degradation, is enclosed in darkness—since to Conrad the very heart of truth is its darkness. In order to allow the Intended to retain the saving innocence of her ideas about Kurtz, Marlow at last determines to tell her a "white lie," thus benevolently keeping her in the dark about the true circumstances of her idealized fiancé's murky death.

In the end, though we cannot deny the symbolic value of light and dark in the tale, the varied "shadings" of reality to which we have been exposed make it impossible to derive any definitive moral signification for that which is light and that dark. All we can be certain of is that their traditional connotations, because they have been thoroughly obfuscated by the context, no longer carry any authority. White may be the cloak of falsehood or evil, blackness the outer covering of truth or goodness. We may usefully recall here the mockingly Christlike appearance that distinguishes the initial guise of the demonic Confidence Man — for while the swindler is presented to us as "a man in cream-colours," whose "flaxen head" is covered by a "fleecy hat" (i.1,2,5), his ivory complexion, we are finally made to recognize, no more symbolizes inner virtue than the appalling "ivory face" of the expiring Kurtz in "Heart of Darkness" (*Youth*, iii.149).

The difficulty of establishing definite meaning for many of the symbols in the two authors speaks for the inconclusiveness both found in human experience. Additional testimony of their belief in life's insolubility is discoverable in the "open form" of their fiction. Although as readers we may often be gratified at the adroit manner in which a literary craftsman draws his story flawlessly to its conclusion, we generally experience no such satisfaction upon finishing a work by Melville or Conrad. For with them, what we are apt to observe is a narrative drawn flawlessly to its *confusion.* The endings of their greatest works suggest their final irresolubility, and, rather than temporarily releasing us from what in life admits of no solution, these works return us directly to these same dilemmas. If it is true that they increase our awareness of the complex and ultimately ungraspable nature of reality, they yet do not provide us with any formula whereby we may better control that reality. Their doubtful resolution leaves us similarly doubtful about our ability to solve life's problems.

Clearly, the frustratingly discordant designs of Melville's and Conrad's best fiction are a technical expression of the two writers' distrust of formal conclusions, a distrust based upon the conviction that whatever small truth was attainable was constantly in flux. If their most compelling works defiantly reject the niceties of the "well-made plot," it is because they are productions of authors whose primary commitment is to the disconnected facts of life and not to the standard formal necessities of a "planned" and "unified" work of art. As Melville put the matter toward the end of *Billy Budd* (discounting his creative restructuring of his sources so that he might forestall criticism for closing his tale inartistically):

> The symmetry of form attainable in pure fiction cannot so readily be achieved in a narration essentially having less to do with fable than with fact. Truth uncompromisingly told will always have its ragged edges; hence the conclusion of such a narration is apt to be less finished than an architectural finial. (xxiv.109)

In attempting to close the gap between reality and literature, Melville consciously organizes his tale to reflect the disharmonies of the real world. Faithful to the disorderly form of life rather than to any artful rearrangement of it, his "unpolished" narrative thus emerges as an unwavering honest rendering of what he as human—rather than as godlike creator—can make of his complex and chaotic world.

There is a similar sense of commitment toward the asymmetrical character of reality in Conrad. For through the indeterminate narratives of Marlow in "Heart of Darkness" and *Lord Jim*, Conrad reveals the circumscribed boundaries to which he as artist is resolved to adhere. When the first speaker of the largely autobiographical "Heart of Darkness" tells us that even before Marlow began his tale, all four men on board the *Nellie* realized they were destined to hear out another one of his "inconclusive experiences," he is indirectly signaling to the reader the necessary irresolution of the tale's close. Especially sensitive to the enigmatic pattern of experience, Marlow is never so glib as to draw final conclusions on characters or events. Kurtz is an "impenetrable darkness" to him and his grasp of Jim's nature strikes him likewise as incomplete and unsatisfactory. But, as he perceptively remarks to his audience of the young romantic, "the last word is not said, — probably shall never be said. Are not our lives too short for that full utterance which through all our stammerings is of course our only and abiding intention?" (*LJ*, xxi.225).

We may note that the equally reflective Ishmael is in much the same position as the ever-searching — and ever-doubtful — Marlow. As Alfred Kazin has pointed out (and here again we may observe how a critical statement about a character of one author may be directly transferred to that of another with a similar creative vision): "For him [Ishmael] nothing is ever finally settled and decided; he is man, or as we like to think, modern man, cut off from the certainty that was once his world. . . . For Ishmael there are no satisfactory conclusions to anything; no final philosophy is ever possible. All that man owns in this world, Ishmael would say [and, we might add, Marlow at one or two points *does* say], is his insatiable mind."[2] The authenticity of Ishmael's and Marlow's narratives, self-consciously artless, almost abortive, furnishes aesthetic validation of "literary openness" as a way for the two authors to express their concept of life. The two narrators themselves, existing *within* a dramatic framework, serve to demonstrate the artistic integrity of the form constructed by their creators from without. Precreative vision merges into created vision as the two writers contrive to make their narrators cogent illustrators of the tale-telling design they feel is most legitimate. As dramatic embodiments of their authors' ideas, both narrators are detached from their creators and, paradoxically, mirror reflections of them; since they do, indeed, speak "directly" for the views they are employed as vehicles to convey.

It is interesting to observe that in *Pierre* — what might be referred to as Melville's "angriest" and least composed novel — the narrator (who in this case is not a dramatically realized creation at all but Melville himself) straightforwardly attacks the intellectually dishonest organization of "pure" fiction. Commenting upon his

---

[2]" 'Introduction' to *Moby-Dick*," in *Melville: A Collection of Critical Essays*, ed. Richard Chase (Englewood Cliffs, New Jersey, 1962), p. 42.

hero's rueful awakening to the unapproachable realities of life, he tells us:

> Like all youths, Pierre had conned his novel-lessons; had read more novels than most persons of his years; but their false, inverted attempts at systematising eternally unsystemisable elements; their audacious, intermeddling impotency, in trying to unravel, and spread out, and classify, the more thin than gossamer threads which make up the complex web of life; these things over Pierre had no power now. Straight through their helpless miserableness he pierced. . . . By infallible presentiment he saw. . .that while the countless tribes of common novels laboriously spin veils of mystery, only to complacently clear them up at last. . .yet the profounder emanations of the human mind, intended to illustrate all that can be humanly known of human life; these never unravel their own intricacies, and have no proper endings, but in imperfect, unanticipated, and disappointing sequels (as mutilated stumps), hurry to abrupt intermergings with the eternal tides of time and fate. (VII.viii.198-199)

In such a tirade as this, the author appears to take the harshest of stands against precisely the sort of novel he must himself have craved to write. For to create "mutilated stumps" in order to keep faith with his deepest vision certainly must have dismayed him. Needing, all the same, to cope actively with the "profounder emanations" of his mind, he is driven to dramatize problems whose solutions he hardly dares propose.

His situation is curiously dramatized in the novel itself by the torn pamphlet containing Plotinus Plinlimmon's lecture. This pamphlet — or more precisely, the part of it accessible to the hero — is entitled *EI* (Greek for "if") and comes to what Melville calls "a most untidy termination" by being ripped off, significantly, directly after the word "if." In these two circumstances, it imitates "formally" the intellectual incompleteness of the novel as a whole. It has, that is, a beginning, middle, and even a kind of conclusion; yet, by remaining provisional and unconcluded, its accumulated meanings are all largely tentative. In another section of commentary, Melville's conclusion about the pamphlet's human value suggests his own discouraged attempts at verbal expression. For he remarks that what he is to give us in his digression concerning Plinlimmon's lecture frankly fails to satisfy "those peculiar motions in my soul, to which that Lecture seems more particularly addressed." But even so, he is reluctant to disparage the lecture, since while it does not finally solve the ethical dilemma it treats, it is an "excellently illustrated re-statement" of this dilemma. Besides, he is aware that though "such mere illustrations are almost universally taken for solutions," it may yet be that "they are the only possible human solutions" (XIV.ii.293).

This viewpoint on man's restricted capacities parallels that of Conrad, whose greatest fiction strives to clarify issues and refuses to clear them up. Perhaps the best example of Conrad's unyielding integrity toward his problematic artistic materials may be found in *Nostromo*, where no system of government is permitted to emerge as a final answer to the political difficulties plaguing the republic of Costaguana. We may, in fact, see in Arnold Kettle's comment on the novel's ending a striking parallel to Melville's attitude toward Plinlimmon's pamphlet. Kettle accurately remarks that Conrad "has no conscious, intellectual solution for the problems of the society" he depicts. But, he adds, "it is foolish to talk glibly of the 'solution' offered by a work of art; the experience of the work of art is in itself a kind of solution, a synthesis, a discovery of the nature of the problem."[3]

Since both Melville and Conrad believed that absolute truth was unknowable, they felt that their aim as novelists should not be to set up a problem and then fashion an artistically coherent solution for it, but rather to work doggedly with some stubbornly resistant question and in so doing suggest its ramifications. Even if in the end they were obliged to leave the question open, they might yet define it with new vividness and force. Matters that could not be neatly resolved might still be satisfactorily explored through a created world designed to accommodate their truest and most

[3]*An Introduction to the English Novel*, II (New York: Harper Torchbook, 1960), 80-81.

unrelenting complexity. Their fiction might, in short, succeed at being infinitely suggestive — which is to say, succeed in achieving the endless reverberations characteristic of great art. Conrad once made explicit his conception of artistic literary expression as almost intrinsically inconclusive and manifold in meaning when he wrote to a correspondent: "a work of art is very seldom limited to one exclusive meaning and not necessarily tending to a definite conclusion. And this for the reason that the nearer it approaches art, the more it acquires a symbolic character."[4] Such a statement hints that literary openness may actually be viewed as a natural by-product of a work's artistry: allowing for no definitive interpretations, it captures the difficult, multisided nature of human experience.

Needless to add, all of Melville's most significant fictions follow Conrad's aesthetic dictum. Similarly questing after moral illumination, they, too, elude all simple critical explanations. For fundamentally they are constructed so as to enable their author to cogitate freely those permanently enigmatic problems with which all artists owe it to their art somehow to come to terms. If these narratives, therefore, like the greatest of Conrad's, are incapable of reaching any ultimate conclusions, it is because their author was forced time after time to confess the final inscrutability of that reality which so intrigued — and mystified — him. Thus the unresolved endings in his work (and in Conrad's as well) can be seen as expressing his refusal to conclude on the essences he dimly perceived.

The occasional reliance upon an elaborate literary style in Melville and Conrad, like their use of formal openness, functions frequently to communicate not the inmost truth of a thing but instead the truth of the two authors' "sensations" with regard to it — at times, even their perplexity over it. Though such rhetoric has sometimes drawn the objection that creative literature should strive for the complete dramatization of its materials and avoid all such things as the "literary essay," the rhetoric of Melville and Conrad does seem, generally, to have a legitimate artistic purpose.

[4]Letter to Barrett H. Clark, 4 May 1918, in *Life and Letters*, II, 205.

That the prose of the two writers *is* sometimes grandiloquent and beyond defense in its straining for effects scarcely needs saying. The overcharged writing to be found in parts of *Mardi, Moby-Dick,* and *Pierre* can hardly be judged as fulfilling a higher aesthetic plan. And the false eloquence too often detectable in Conrad's Malayan novels and in his first volume of short stories also seems artistically unjustifiable. It is difficult, for instance, not to see as rhetorically overdrawn a description of nature proclaiming that "immense forests, hiding fateful complications of fantastic life, lay in the eloquent silence of mute greatness" ("An Outpost of Progress," *Tales of Unrest,* i.94). Such "Conradese" does not, of course, deserve to be taken very seriously. When we move to the rhetoric of "Heart of Darkness," however, we may appreciate in Marlow's propensity for what must at first strike us as suspiciously "literary" vocalizations an honest attempt to render the way a thing is sensed. Here rhetoric is used not to overpower the reader with the idea that the enormity of the reality depicted defies straightforward expression, but rather to suggest broadly the *impression* that a thing might evoke. By its loyalty to the perceiver's immediate reactions, such abstract diction might succeed in transmitting the truth of the subjective. When Marlow tries to account for his response to Kurtz's high-strung and highly moving report on the savages by telling his auditors: "It gave me the notion of an exotic Immensity ruled by an august Benevolence" (*Youth,* ii.118), it should be evident that his own rhetoric is neither gratuitous nor insincere. For it vigorously conveys his "unreal" reaction in momentarily coming under the spell of Kurtz's eloquence.

Besides the use of rhetoric to relate "the truth of one's own sensations" (and such a device is admittedly far more often found in Conrad than in Melville), rhetoric might be employed to intimate what could never be known, and because of this, never dramatized. Though, for example, Melville might have wished his Confidence Man to symbolize not only the archetypal trickster but Satan as well, his conviction that truth could not be derived from appearances made it impossible for him to expose his villain outright.

His solution, consequently, was to hint at his central character's inward nature through a descriptive language that, although seemingly innocent, was contrived to divulge *metaphorically* the fraud's true identity. When, for instance, the swindler is seeking to insinuate himself into the confidence of the college student, Melville pictures him as "softly sliding nearer" to the collegian and "with the softest air, quivering down and looking up" (*C-M*, v.34). The author's own cunning, it should be noted, enables him to transcend the radical limitations of his narrative perspective, which is itself restricted to surface reality.

Having schooled himself, as has been mentioned earlier, on writers such as Flaubert, Maupassant, and James, Conrad, too, was skeptical about the artistic validity of direct authorial interpretation. Still, his feeling that the deepest truths resisted dramatization made him aware of the occasional necessity of narrative commentary if the author were to communicate accurately his point of view. His final ambivalence over the whole situation may be inferred from a letter to F. N. Doubleday in which, discussing specifically the idea of a writer's answering his critics in print, he remarked: ". . .I think that an author who tries to 'explain' is exposing himself to a very great risk of confessing himself a failure. For a work of art should speak for itself. Yet much could be said on the other side; for it is also clear that a work of art is not a logical demonstration carrying its intention on the face of it."[5] There are times in Conrad's own writing when a self-consciously literary use of language is adopted in an almost desperate attempt to suggest the complicated tensions of the inner truth, which the reader otherwise might not be able to appreciate. One notable example of this studied exploitation of language may be observed in *Lord Jim*, where Marlow, speaking of Jim's manner in Patusan, reflects that "he seemed to love the land and the people with a sort of fierce egoism, with a contemptuous tenderness" (xxiv.248). With Kurtz, Marlow's language is frequently even more theoretical, for Kurtz is not so much "one of us" as he is an "impenetrable darkness."

[5] 2 June 1924, in *Life and Letters*, II, 344.

If Marlow must depend heavily on rhetoric in telling us about Kurtz, it is because his subject remains so insubstantial to him. Only his voice seems material, and this is so not because Marlow finds his speech particularly convincing, but because it is articulated in tones that most effectively reverberate in his ears. Thus his sensation of Kurtz can be brought out *only* rhetorically. It is, in fact, unlikely that a naturalistic description of the man's inflated utterances could come as near to disclosing the essential truth about him.

Meville's artistic motives, like Conrad's, are calculated to give the reader a glimpse of inner reality. But true to the mode of man's apprehension, he presents us with "spectacles" (a word used with special point in "Benito Cereno") that belie this reality. Because appearances are in the end illusory, only through resorting to rhetoric, or—as in the case of "Benito Cereno"—to a direct presentation of the facts, might the author suggest something resembling the true state of affairs. Even here, however, since in no case is ultimate reality perceptible, Melville (and Conrad, too) often felt obliged to fall back on such metaphysically congenial adjectives as "elusive" or "inscrutable." The ponderous diction of both authors, particularly as it is employed "dramatically" through the narrators Ishmael and Marlow, may thus be seen as expressive of their profoundest theme: the insoluble mystery of experience. Properly considered, such a motif defies rhetorical as well as dramatic expression; as a result, when the implications of an episode become murky, so, eventually, does the prose. Concrete description lapses into indefinite suggestiveness as the object of perception drops irretrievably out of focus. Rhetoric, having served its function of intimating what could not be shown, emerges itself as an implicit—at times, even *explicit*—admission of the author's own inability to grasp the essence of his subject.

Melville and Conrad's realization of man's cognitively limited relationship to the world provides the philosophic vindication for their abandonment of the omniscient narrative perspective in their fiction and the adoption of a correspondingly limited point of view.

Since all the reality a man might know was shaped by his own consciousness rather than bestowed upon him from the outside, both authors chose to center their artistic lens not on some intuited objective reality, but on the immediate human sources for any of the infinite realities man might, in effect, "create" according to his own individual temperament. From yet another direction, then, we note the artistic preferences growing out of the two authors' nihilism.

The works that best exemplify Melville's predilection for the drastically limited point of view are "Bartleby," "Benito Cereno," and *The Confidence-Man*. Each tale is rigidly confined to a single, highly restricted narrative perspective (with the partial exception of "Benito Cereno"). Further, there are no informants or confidants present to disclose information crucial to our understanding; only the narrator is available to guess at what is signified by the mystifying characters and events. And either the narrator is so pragmatic as to be impossibly removed from his subject (as is the attorney in "Bartleby"), intentionally deceptive (as is the hedging narrator of "Benito Cereno"), or exasperatingly tongue in cheek (as is the habitually qualifying narrator of *The Confidence-Man*). The impressionistic point of view common to all these works is not, we must conclude, a means of getting to reality, but only a means of demonstrating that reality cannot be gotten to at all. This circumstance explains, for instance, why we can never confidently interpret Bartleby: brought to life as he is wholly by one who must confess his inability to understand him, there is no way that we can sketch in his form so as to discern at last "the essential Bartleby." The scanty materials we must work with make it impossible to complete the fragmentary portrait that confounds us.

"Benito Cereno" is perhaps the most remarkable of all Melville's fictions in its employment of a point of view calculated to illustrate perceptual nearsightedness. Here the predominant concern (as usual in the author) is with the eventual bringing forth of a hidden reality. But here once again the narrative lens through which events are refracted serves only to obfuscate the inward reality that seems to glow so tantalizingly beneath the shaded world of appearances. And so Melville's art, attempting at once to maintain faith with the imprisoning structures of life and to derive artistically valid significations from them, ends up not by disclosing the inner truth of events but by distinguishing subjective, knowable reality from *absolute* reality—the latter postulated as alone having value, the former acknowledged as alone accessible to man. "Benito Cereno" conveys this hopeless message to us first by narrating the happenings on board the *San Dominick* as they are viewed by a man whose good nature and charitable disposition place the objects of his perception forever beyond his apprehension; and then by becoming "objective" and giving us excerpts from the court depositions of this most treacherous case. For neither of these perspectives on Don Benito's confrontation with the Negro yields the reality we seek. Both narrative techniques—by carefully formulated artistic design—"succeed in failing" to extract essential meaning from the materials they so scrupulously render. By presenting us with the two poles of realism in point of view, Melville thus manages to expose the insubstantiality of both, and also to insinuate, paradoxically, that such perspectives are the only "substantial" ones at man's disposal. Recalling Ishmael, he but puts the brow of reality before us, implicitly defying us to read its inner significance (see *M-D,* II.1xxix.83).

Unlike Melville, Conrad tends to stress his concept of an unknowable reality not by staunchly maintaining a circumscribed point of view, but, ironically, by devising multiple narrative perspectives whereby to explore his subject more efficiently. In the end, however, his narrative devices are complementary to Melville's. And while Marlow, in terms of his ability to perceive, may be diametrically opposite the short-sighted Delano, Kurtz emerges as not much less of an enigma to him than does Don Benito to the American Captain. Conrad's thesis, then, is identical to Melville's in its ultimately rejecting the possibility of piercing the reality of which one is spectator. The generalizations to which Marlow's contact with the depraved Kurtz may justifiably give rise are nonetheless generalizations, insufficient to enable him to feel that he has learned his subject's deepest secret. It may not be irrelevant to point out, as William York Tindall already has, that the roving and occasionally omniscient voice that gives us *The Nigger of the "Narcissus,"* himself looks ahead to Marlow "in his devotion to simile, his moral anxiety, his delight in 'enigma,' and his surrender to 'the fascination of the incomprehensible.' "[6] As such, we might add, he also looks backward to Melville's Ishmael, who is similarly fascinated by what he recognizes as beyond his mortal capacities to comprehend.

It might appear that in *Lord Jim* Conrad wished to place Marlow in a position intellectually superior to the one he held in "Heart of Darkness"; for here the author sees fit to provide his bemused narrator with a variety of informants whose facts and feelings about the central subject would seem, collectively, to afford Marlow with some final criteria by which to understand—and judge—Jim's conduct. At least the availability of a wide range of points of view toward the youth *should* add up to something, we are inclined to think. But we are eventually made aware that multiple perspectives are of no more avail than a single isolated point of view, when the nature of the inquiry has nothing to do with verifiable facts but with basic truths. So long as each perspective on Jim is relative and dependent on personal impression (as it must be in the absence of an all-knowing narrator who presumes to fit events into some prescribed framework of meaning), Jim's essence must remain unfathomable, even to one as morally sensitive and subtle as Marlow. Through the narrator's different confidants, we may learn more and more about Jim, but whatever comes to light about him can be interpreted in such a multitude of ways that at no point are we capable of ascertaining the objective reality of his being.

In a seriocomic but not altogether crude manner, the opening of *Moby-Dick* may itself be understood as purposefully adopting multiple perspectives toward its subject. In order to help us derive

[6]"Apology for Marlow," in *Conrad's "Heart of Darkness" and the Critics,* ed. Bruce Harkness (Belmont, Calif., 1960), p. 126.

the essence of the whale, the author supplies us with definitions of him, a wide assortment of names given to him by different countries and civilizations, and finally a whole host of quotations, literary and otherwise, that make him their subject. But while the "etymology" and "extracts" with which we are abundantly furnished definitely succeed in imparting to us a keen *sense* of the whale (as Marlow's narratives do with respect to Kurtz and Jim), they stop short of "resolving" his meaning.

The theme of inscrutability in Melville and Conrad emerges most pointedly, perhaps, through the use of certain techniques of suspense, which, unlike the traditional suspense story, are never fully relieved by a detective who brilliantly solves the case and handily divides the innocent from the guilty. Probably the most outstanding "mysteries" in the two writers are Melville's "Benito Cereno" and Conrad's *Lord Jim*, and in both these works the puzzled reader's enlightenment comes primarily in his being made to understand all that will *always* be puzzling to him.

If in "Benito Cereno" Melville chooses to give us only as much of the events on board the *San Dominick* as Captain Delano is capable of making out, it is because he does not wish to divulge what may remain well concealed to an observer. As we learn from the court extracts, one of the reasons that Amasa Delano is unable to grasp the tragically reversed position of the whites and blacks on the Spaniard's ship has to do with all "the devices which offered contradictions to the true state of affairs" (*The Piazza Tales*, p. 164). The machinations of the Negroes disguise reality, and Melville, faithful to his conception of inward reality as inaccessible to the spectator, shrewdly determines to take various opportunities to encourage the reader to trust the good will of the appearances presented him. At the least, he asks the reader to suspend his suspicions until the narrative clears up what must naturally strike him as peculiar. From this aspect, technique and theme are so tightly interwoven that they cannot be separated without undoing the author's elaborate creative pattern.

Despite the plenitude of studies on "Benito Cereno," Melville's greatest tour de force, almost nothing has been said about the author's very conscious attempts to cajole the reader into reposing his sympathy in Delano's faulty perspective.[7] Unquestionably, in striving to be true to Delano's angle of vision, Melville is often intentionally false to the reader by screening through his commentary the true state of affairs. For one thing, the nondramatized narrator of the tale—although he is to be distinguished in his perception from Delano—generally adheres to the same narrow point of view. Speaking in a confiding, matter-of-fact way, he designs either to win our confidence or mitigate our mistrust by indulging in seemingly innocent "digressions," craftily planned to maintain our belief in a reality that, in fact, is monstrously deceptive. For instance, there are the passages that are aimed in the most unassuming way to make us better understand the endearing qualities of the Negro servant, indirectly predisposing us to regard the villainous Babo positively. To consider only a single example, we might take the narrator's "disinterested" observation on Babo's devoted attendance to Don Benito's needs:

> Sometimes the negro gave his master his arm, or took his handkerchief out of his pocket for him; performing these and similar offices with that affectionate zeal which transmutes into something filial or fraternal acts in themselves but menial; and which has gained for the negro the repute of making the most pleasing body servant in the world; one, too, whom a master need be on no stiffly superior terms with, but may treat with familiar trust; less a servant than a devoted companion. (p. 75)

Prompted to take the black Babo "liberally" to our hearts, we are also—to complicate matters further—inclined to suspend our doubts about Don Benito, arising from his eccentric treatment both of his Negroes and of Captain Delano's friendly offices. For the narrator, charitably disposed toward everyone, chooses at one point

---

[7]See, however, Mary Rohrberger, "Point of View in 'Benito Cereno': Machinations and Deceptions," *College English*, XXVII (1966), 541-546.

to anticipate the tale's conclusion by assuring us that Delano's periodic uncertainty about the Spaniard's integrity is, however understandable, actually unjustified. After Delano has at one point succeeded in dispelling his suspicions regarding Don Benito's baffling reserve toward him, we are told that "lightly humming a tune, [he] now began indifferently pacing the poop, so as not to betray to Don Benito that he had at all mistrusted incivility, much less duplicity; for such mistrust would yet be proved illusory, and by the event; though, for the present, the circumstance which had provoked that distrust remained unexplained" (p. 93). Using our hindsight, we can detect the significance such a strangely reassuring, and yet finally mystifying, description has in deluding the reader. The deepest irony to be emphasized here is that the ostensibly reliable narrator is throughout so equivocating and disinclined to pass negative judgments on *any* of the characters that Delano's own credulity is not only made to impress us at certain moments as "reasonable," but as, indeed, a trifle tainted with cynicism. When the narrator's beguiling voice finally gives way to the reportorial presentation of the "inner" facts elucidating the baffling actions we could not otherwise explain, we learn the necessity of suspecting everything until its inward nature has been clarified for us. This is the "lesson" that the tale is bent on teaching us, and its success depends on our first being "taken in" by the author himself. Our own credulity must be exploited so that we may learn, in the recognition of its betrayal, its tenuous foundation. It should be evident that the Melville of *The Confidence-Man* has much the same point in mind when he arranges for his narrator to stand silently by while the trickster-hero bombards us with specious arguments for placing our confidence in nature, man, and God.

The Marlow of *Lord Jim* is not, of course, so insidious a narrator as are those of "Benito Cereno" and *The Confidence-Man*. Still, the truthful Englishman — through shifts in chronology and perspective, through digressions, and through a most leisurely narrative method generally — contrives to evoke a feeling of suspense and uncertainty toward the central subject. His narrative technique is reminiscent of "Benito Cereno" in its willfully holding back crucial information (most notably the fact that the endangered *Patna* did *not* in the end sink at all). The result of this devious manner of exposition is that the reader is himself obliged to piece the facts of the story together if he is to make some overall sense of them. In order to orient himself properly as one of Marlow's audience, he is driven to concentrate more and more carefully on the reality slowly unfolding before him. All the same, he is not permitted by the narrator to gain a vivid perception of that reality, and is constantly forced to evaluate and reevaluate the evidence that, in one way or another, turns up in the course of Marlow's own quest for underlying meaning. As more and more is revealed to him, he may attain an increasingly greater awareness of the facts surrounding Jim; but, as we have pointed out earlier, since all such facts have their existence *outside* of Jim, they are never adequate to disclose the inner truth of him.

The novel's narrative system, then, seems especially devised to take us to the most "privileged" human distance — not the distance at which ultimate truths stand naked before us, but rather where we may perceive them, paradoxically, as forever out of sight. As in "Benito Cereno," the book's impressionistic point of view serves to express its theme of final inscrutability. Since Albert Guerard in his *Conrad the Novelist* has remarked significantly on the similarities of Melville's novella to Conrad's novel, we may conclude our discussion of the two works by emphasizing his important observation that impressionistic novels such as these (and also Faulkner's *Absalom, Absalom!*) require a second reading if a full (or at least fuller) understanding of them is to be reached. For on rereading:

> The mere factual mysteries are solved, and no longer preoccupy us. . . . But now by the same token we can watch the drama of moral ambiguity as such, and the mechanisms of deception; and can watch the observers or narrators of the action, their mistakes, their withheld or grudging commitments. The human situation

becomes more rather than less complex. Yet we are at the same time freer to observe art as art: the game of management and grouping and perspective.[8]

The end result of the limited narrative perspective in Melville and Conrad is that the empirical approach to life replaces the abstractly intuitive one. If both authors show a reluctance to dramatize their materials, to create a truly dramatic scene in the manner of Dickens or Dostoevsky, this circumstance may be attributed, at least in part, to the incompatibility of their impressionistic techniques with the absolute objectification requisite to the dramatic mode. Their desire to stress the relative nature of reality inclines them to treat persons and things not so much as discrete entities, but as objects to be animated by an individual's temperament and capacity for perception. We may recall most conveniently "The Doubloon" chapter in *Moby-Dick*, where each spectator of the equatorial coin sees no more than what it is in him to see. As Ahab remarks: "this round gold is but the image of the rounder globe, which, like a magician's globe, to each and every man in turn but mirrors back his own mysterious self" (II.xcix.190). And Ahab's subjectivism is echoed in Pip's apparently meaningless pronouncement: "I look, you look, he looks; we look, ye look, they look" (p. 194). Ironically, the now crazed Pip—who, Ishmael tells us, is in possession of heavenly sense, having lost his earthly sanity (see II.xciii.170)—is able, because of the very disappearance of his former, individualized self, to regard objectively the subjectivity of every man's interpretation of that which confronts him. His statement implies the indefinitely broad range of views attendant upon exposing a single object to any number of sensibilities, either individually or in combination. Thus are we made to glimpse the limits of man's perception, limits that prevent all his conclusions from attaining the status of absolute truth.

---

[8]Cambridge, Mass., 1958, p. 130. See also p. 126, where Guerard equates "Benito Cereno" and *Lord Jim* in their "minute control of the reader's responses to ambiguity."

The impossibility of achieving objective knowledge about anything, which constitutes the intellectual basis for the two authors' employment of a subjective point of view, has the effect not only of distancing the narrator from the subject he pursues, but of defining him (or his search) as itself the tale's subject of investigation. On this level, we may regard Ishmael, in his vigorous undertakings to discover imaginatively the meaning of Ahab and the whale, as thematically central in *Moby-Dick*; we may see the attorney of "Bartleby," in his frustrated efforts to understand and, if possible, accommodate his enigmatic scrivener, as himself rendering the meaning of insolubility around which the tale revolves; we may perceive the imperceptive Captain Delano, in his ineffectual attempts to make out the reality confronting him, as the story's key interest rather than Don Benito's tragic experience; and, lastly, we may recognize the Melville of *Billy Budd,* in his unrelenting endeavors to ascertain the meaning and value of his tale and characters, as himself the focal point of that moral-intellectual drama.

In most of Conrad's important works also, instead of being *given* a principal character (as Sophocles gives us an Oedipus or Shakespeare a Hamlet), we are presented with a narrator in conscientious search of his subject, who, by refusing to "reveal" himself, resolutely resists the narrator's spotlight. In default, as it were, the narrator's very failure to throw adequate light on his subject becomes crucial to the story, which must, in consequence, be recognized as ultimately "untellable." Because man's heart is so dark, Marlow in "Heart of Darkness" must confess his inability to penetrate Kurtz and rest what little hope remains to him in the possibility of penetrating a little deeper into his own half-obscured nature. As he notes: "The most you can hope from [life] is some knowledge of yourself" (*Youth*, iii.150). The self-quest that in the end is to be seen as Marlow's primary and abiding concern is similarly discernible in *Lord Jim.* It is, in fact, Marlow's uncertainty about his potentialities that most draws him to Jim, whose own character he finds so difficult to determine. He himself is prepared to confess: "I cannot say I had ever seen [Jim] distinctly. . .but it seemed to me that the less I understood the more I was bound to him in the name of that doubt which is the inseparable part of our knowledge. I did not know so much more about myself" (xxi.221). Turning momentarily to Melville, we cannot but be struck by the relationship such a description of the narrator's magnetic attraction to the unfortunate youth has with the almost perverse fascination of the attorney-narrator in "Bartleby" for his hapless scrivener. For both Jim and Bartleby are vaguely conceived by the narrators who breathe life into them as frighteningly viable "realizations" of their own hidden selves. If Marlow were to exclaim at one point: "Ah Jim! ah humanity!" we might interpret his aroused utterance faithfully by recalling that he is forced to regard Jim as "one of us"—just as the attorney, recognizing a double in his now useless employee, must admit fraternally: "both I and Bartleby were sons of Adam" (*The Piazza Tales*, p. 40). In addition, Marlow's justification of his frequently self-centered method of telling Jim's story accurately accounts for the somewhat "off-focused" quality of the attorney's narrative of Bartleby. For, Marlow informs us,

> I am telling you so much about my own instinctive feelings and bemused reflections because there remains so little to be told of him. He existed for me, and after all it is only through me that he exists for you. I've led him out by the hand; I have paraded him before you. (*LJ*, xxi.224)

The titular characters of a "Bartleby" or a *Lord Jim* do not, we must conclude, warrant being viewed independently as the principals of their respective dramas. For, figuratively, they emerge on stage holding hands with their impresarios; and as a result they can "lead" their dramas only as they are led to lead them. Conrad's title *Under Western Eyes* may be seen as a most explicit admission of the biased point of view through which we get Razumov, the Russian whom the teacher-narrator never quite feels sure he can grasp. The (to him) alien nature of Razumov's temperament is symbolic generally of the insurmountable difficulties that Conrad's scrupulous tale-tellers have in "objectifying" their subjects. And yet we as readers, given only their perspective and factual resources to operate with, must also be puzzled at appearances that connote no certain reality. Eventually, we are prompted to divide our attention between the protagonist and what the narrator makes of him. The conclusion that typically suggests itself from our split response to the narrative is that no definite meaning is ever ascribable to the object perceived. Finally, all we are left with is the narrator's consciousness — and our own. If through the authors' continued psychological probings we are at least made more aware of human nature — and of the immortal human condition as well — we may rightfully conclude that the only legitimate "meaning" the narrative could hold has been communicated effectively. For the relativism of its point of view allows no convenient message or moral. A metaphysic denying the possibility of completely apprehending anything can provide no basis for establishing meaningful patterns amid life's chaotic drift. The limited narrative viewpoint, then, like all the other techniques we have discussed in the fiction of Melville and Conrad, can be interpreted as an aesthetic consequence of the two authors' abiding belief in inscrutability.

CHAPTER V

THE DILEMMA OF "HOW TO BE" AND THE LEAP TO VALUES

The lucidity that prevented Melville and Conrad from maintaining any confident belief also made it difficult for them to suggest in their fiction a more satisfactory way of life than those they exposed as inadequate. Their insights, they recognized, were far more likely to raise unanswerable questions than to resolve merely puzzling ones; and their skepticism about human solutions was far better adapted to rejecting a mode of behavior than to recommending an alternative.

Since the truth of nihilism was fundamentally the truth of nothingness, both writers were alarmed by the perilousness of their ideas. Courageous enough to acknowledge the darkness at the vital center of things, they yet understood the hazards of structuring life according to such a view. To be constantly aware of life's essential obscurity was to dwell fearfully close to the "horror," and so, they realized, it might often be advisable to shun truth as though it were falsehood. Marlow in "Heart of Darkness" may be questing for inward reality, but when he makes his perilous trip to Kurtz and the Inner Station, and is made to glimpse the hideous gloom of this reality, he counts himself fortunate to be able to immerse himself in the details of his captainship. The primordial lawlessness and abandon that he dimly perceives in himself through his contact with primitive African life makes him turn to his tedious duties on the steamer almost with relief. For he realizes that he can best evade the psychic threat of the Congo by concentrating solely on the practical problems of keeping his dilapidated boat above water. As he notes: "When you have to attend to things of that sort, to the mere incidents of the surface, the reality—the reality, I tell you—fades. The inner truth is hidden—luckily, luckily" (*Youth*, ii.93). And a few pages later Conrad has him add: "There was surface-truth enough in these things to save a wiser man" (ii.97). The point here, of course, is that essential truth, by having far more to do with amoral chaos than with ethical order, may fatally endanger the civilized routines man has so tirelessly cultivated in order to live in some semblance of peace.

Insofar as truth destroyed one's equanimity and made life more arduous rather than less, it was to be scrupulously avoided. In *The Secret Agent*, Conrad tells us that Winnie Verloc is "confirmed in her instinctive conviction that things don't bear looking into very much" (viii.180), and it is interesting that he hardly feels within his rights to condemn this veritable cult of ignorance. For such stolidity might stave off that knowledge which menaces the only sort of life ordinary mortals are fit for. The novel itself dramatically verifies the sustaining value of Winnie's ignorance by illustrating the fatal consequences attendant upon her at last being obliged to see everything she would have much preferred not to see at all. In *Victory*, Heyst's deceased father is presented to us as a nihilistic thinker—a man who has seen into life's darkness and written many books so that others, too, might see it, and thereby liberate themselves from the unreasonable illusions binding them. But Conrad, by informing us that "the world. . .had instinctively rejected his wisdom" (II.iii.91), suggests unequivocally that the philosopher's truth is intolerable to the general public.

Because Melville's deepest truths were also dark and disruptive, he was fearful of giving them explicit expression in his writing and thus offending his readership. As Henry Murray has noted: "Perhaps the broadest generalization that can be made about Melville's different Truths is that they are *all* culturally unacceptable."[1] So while the author might at times have wished, like his wildly declaiming Pierre, to decry "the detested and distorted images of all the convenient lies and duty-subterfuges of the diving and ducking moralities of this earth" (V.vi.150), he had to confess the recklessness of such a project. For the attempt at systematic propagation of a point of view utterly incompatible with popularly held beliefs could lead only to censure—as both Pierre's fate and, indeed, the fate of *Pierre* testify. To Hawthorne, Melville once wrote: ". . .Truth is the silliest thing under the sun. Try to get a living by the Truth—and go to the Soup Societies. Heavens! Let any clergyman try to preach the Truth from its very stronghold, the pulpit, and they would ride him out of his church on his own pulpit bannister."[2] Conrad's half-mocking tone toward Heyst's unreservedly truthful father reveals the same ironic awareness of the imprudence of trying to communicate a view of reality completely at odds with society's most cherished illusions of it. For man cannot bear to have his fragile convictions shaken by the rough force of logic, and may therefore be expected to react with self-righteous hostility to all assaults on his unquestioned—and, to him, unquestionable—beliefs.

It is surely revelatory that one of the things which most attracted Melville to Shakespeare was his intuition that the dramatist shared his own cautious hesitation about uttering truth. Charles Olson, who in his researches on Melville took the opportunity to investigate the author's personal copy of Shakespeare's plays, informs us that

> when Shakespeare muzzles truth-speakers, Melville is quick to mark the line or incident. In *Antony and Cleopatra* he puts a check besides Enobarbus' blunt answer to Antony's correction of his speech: "That truth should be silent I had almost forgot."
>
> In *Lear* he underscores the Fool's answer to Lear's angry threat of the whip: "Truth's a dog must to kennel; he must be whipp'd out, when Lady the brach may stand by th' fire and stink."[3]

[1] "Introduction" to *Pierre*, pp. xxix-xxx.
[2] 1? June 1851, in *Letters*, p. 127.
[3] *Call Me Ishmael* (New York, 1947), p. 42.

In his essay "Hawthorne and His Mosses," Melville explains his admiration for Shakespeare by speaking of him as a master of the "great Art of Telling the Truth." But he realizes that Shakespeare was obliged to do this "covertly, and by snatches," for "in this world of lies, Truth is forced to fly like a scared white doe in the woodlands; and only by cunning glimpses will she reveal herself." When we think of the devious devices by which Melville contrived in his own fictions to disclose life's deepest truths, we can surmise the affinity he felt toward his fellow "truth teller." Recognizing the prohibitive cost of unrestrained sincerity, he sensed the necessity of an author's "turning over" his profoundest thoughts to one of his dramatis personae. As he put it in the same essay:

> Through the mouths of the dark characters of Hamlet, Timon, Lear, and Iago, he craftily says, or sometimes, insinuates, the things which we feel to be so terrifically true that it were all but madness for any good man, in his own proper character, to utter, or even hint of them. Tormented into desperation, Lear the frantic king tears off the mask, and speaks the sane madness of vital truth.

Conrad's remark in *The Rescue*, that "the world is too prudent to be sincere" (III.vi.151), can doubtless be seen as complementing Melville's feeling that absolute truthfulness was a "sanely mad" position to adopt. In addition, the comparative shallowness of much of Conrad's later—and, significantly, most popular—fiction suggests the high price of *artistic* integrity recognizable in the author's earlier—and far less remunerative—work; it may even offer one explanation of his eventual fictional abandonment of his darker, truer—and far less "marketable"—vision. Melville's complete withdrawal from his career as novelist thirty-four years before his death provides further evidence of the well-nigh forbidding cost of engaging oneself full-scale in the art of telling the truth.

If it was uncircumspect to try to communicate the knowledge of life's inner darkness, it was also unwise to pursue this truth very far on one's own. We have already quoted Melville's warning in

Pierre that "the trail of truth" had better not be followed beyond a certain point, and the novel itself can be seen as demonstrating the folly of the hero's uncompromising quest for essential meaning. Just as Marlow recognizes the saving qualities of "surface truth," so is Pierre eventually forced to realize the damning nature of what we might call "secret truth." His final evaluation of his idealistic search for ultimates that might enable him to live meaningfully records his horrible sense of self-victimization. For at last in possession of the most fearful lucidity man may attain, he must proclaim himself "the fool of Truth, the fool of Virtue, the fool of Fate" (XXVI.iv.499). Much like Taji and Ahab before him, and Benito Cereno and Bartleby afterwards, he is defeated by his exceptional, and "unorthodox," sensitivity—a sensitivity that allows him to perceive man's soul as "appallingly vacant [and] vast" (see XXI.i.397). In Conrad, such characters as Kurtz, Jim, and Decoud provide additional examples of the hazards born of the individualist attempt to "follow one's dream," or at least to look more intently into one's self than is typical—or, for that matter, advisable. Perhaps Pierre is most comparable to Kurtz in that, like Kurtz, he "step[s] over the threshold of the invisible" ("HD," *Youth*, iii.151), and encounters a darkness that nullifies in its obscurity all of man's ethical propositions, and thus the very foundation of civilized existence.

Because the discovery of the heart of darkness cannot profitably be communicated to others nor easily adjusted to one's own spiritual needs, the fate of man initiated into truth is, as we might expect, almost uniformly negative in the two writers. To be introduced to life's emptiness was to become alienated from one's fellow-man and to forfeit the reassurances indispensable to contented living. After Benito Cereno's disastrous encounter with blackness, he can no longer relate to the outside world, and the morbid isolation that is the effect of his unreconcilable knowledge leads him directly to the grave. Bartleby's diseased sense of the mockery that is life also has a fatal conclusion—and, looking back to Ahab and Pierre, we may observe how the two characters' perception of what is either "inscrutably malicious" or "appallingly vacant" leads them toward social withdrawal and eventually toward death itself.

In Conrad, too, initiation into the gloom of darkness imperils one's feeling of relatedness to others and, at times, his mortal welfare. Marlow's experience with Kurtz's ultimate vacancy may bring him closer to understanding the soul of man, but it also functions to distance him from the human community. Society's life-sustaining illusions can never again quell the anxiety that his penetrating view of Kurtz and savage African life has instilled in him. In *Victory*, the disenchanting upbringing that causes Heyst to violate his nature and attempt, futilely, to break with the world is finally responsible for the world's defeat of him. Skeptical about entering into life's masquerade and unable to convince himself of the sense of any self-assertive plan of action whatever, he is incapable of defending himself when his very life is at stake. Decoud, too, is given to us as "a victim of the disillusioned weariness which is the retribution meted out to intellectual audacity" (*Nostromo*, III.x.501). When his physical isolation on the Golfo Placido augments his radical lack of belief, his suicide is the inevitable result. Having to face the world's stubborn silence in unrelieved solitude, he ultimately loses all supporting sense of a personal identity and, like Benito Cereno, can look forward in his painful unrest only to the peace that is death.

The only character in either of the two authors actually able to capitalize upon his lucidity would appear to be Melville's Confidence Man. Here is a person who, without faith himself, has learned how to exploit his nihilistic awareness most satisfyingly by betraying others to repose their faith in him.[4] Both his success as a swindler and his complacent attitude toward human existence (which he regards amusedly as "a pic-nic *en costume*" [xxiv.178]), indicate the possibility of perceiving life's void and, surreptitiously

<hr/>

[4]For a detailed discussion of the nihilistic undercurrents in *The Confidence-Man*, and also of the exceptional lucidity of the book's swindler-hero, see Leon F. Seltzer, "Camus's Absurd and the World of Melville's *Confidence-Man*," *PMLA*, LXXXII (March 1967), 14-27.

winking at it, going on to assume a personally gratifying role in it. Still, the immoral part that the Confidence Man plays so triumphantly hardly suggests a satisfactory way of living one's nihilism, since the trickster's actions *are* ethically unacceptable—whether or not that ethic has any absolute justification. What *The Confidence-Man* seems to imply, then, is that accommodating life to one's beliefs is at once self-indulgent and terrifyingly inconsiderate of one's fellow-man. Melville's obviously "comic" solution to the existential dilemma posed in *Mardi, Moby-Dick, Pierre,* "Bartleby," and "Benito Cereno" must therefore be deemed unacceptable, just as the problem these other works so diligently handle is unsolvable.

If adapting to life's bleakest truth is so difficult a task, it follows that for one to disclose such truth to another willfully is an act of the most unfeeling cruelty. It is bad enough to be initiated into the darkness oneself without righteously trying to introduce others to its jarring force, and both authors are explicit in expressing their conviction that the inner reality of life had best be concealed from those "luckily" unaware of it. When Pierre has privately learned about his father's French mistress and deliberates on whether to disclose the disenchanting facts to his mother so that Isabel, the illegitimate and now abandoned product of that early illicit affair, may be admitted to the Glendinning household, he is made to recognize both the heartlessness and futility of such an undertaking. For not only was it unlikely that his haughty mother would agree to shelter such a waif, but it was also quite possible that for her to be so shockingly disillusioned in her husband's virtue would make her life unbearable. Melville, wishing to convince us of the inhumanity of telling the truth under these circumstances, notes that

> through Pierre's mind there then darted a baleful thought; how that the truth should not always be paraded; how that sometimes a lie is heavenly, and truth infernal. Filially infernal, truly, thought Pierre, if I should by one vile breath of truth, blast my father's blessed memory in the bosom of my mother, and plant the sharpest dagger of grief in her soul. I will not do it! (V.ii.128)

This passage may help to explicate the closing scene of "Heart of Darkness," since Marlow's reasons for withholding from Kurtz's Intended the terrible truth of her former fiance's moral failing are identical to those Pierre professes. As Marlow briefly but suggestively concludes: "I could not tell her. It would have been too dark—too dark altogether" (*Youth*, iii.162). As an alternative, therefore, he kindly decides to deceive her with a "heavenly lie," an untruth that will keep intact her treasured illusions about Kurtz. Thus are we indirectly made to appreciate how Melville and Conrad's basic compassion prevented them from advocating the transmission of truths possibly disastrous to the one informed.

At one point or another, the specific dilemma of handling truth merges with the general dilemma of handling one's whole existence; for once a person has glimpsed the darker meanings belying all conventionally accepted formulas of conduct, he loses the vital reassurances provided by society's protective framework of illusion. Although the idealist in Melville and Conrad may be sensitive enough to formulate his values apart from society, he almost invariably fails because he lacks the sensitivity to perceive the inadequacies both in his substitute values and in himself. Some of the difficulties of trying to live on a loftier plane than one's fellow-man are summed up in Plotinus Plinlimmon's pamphlet, where the distinction between chronometrical (absolute) and horological (relative) time is made by way of pointing out the essential incompatibility of celestial and worldly wisdom. Since man is flawed by nature, any attempt he may make to live in agreement with chronometrical time is predestined to failure. The uncompromising standards that he adopts in order to perfect himself may lead him in fact to compromise himself. As Plinlimmon stresses (and his words foretell Pierre's sad fate): "almost invariably, with inferior beings, the absolute effort to live in this world according to the strict letter of the chronometricals is, somehow, apt to involve those inferior beings eventually in strange, *unique* follies and sins, unimagined before" (XIV.iii.296). The obstinate and unheeding pursuit of an ideal is all too likely to result in that ideal's corruption, as not only the case of Pierre testifies, but also Taji's idealized quest for Yillah and Ahab's self-righteous hunt for the leviathan. All three characters, in glorifying their capacities as human beings, finally renounce their humanity altogether. Taji's pertinacity in his mad search causes him eventually to forsake the world; Ahab's horrible relentlessness culminates in the drowning of virtually his whole crew; and Pierre's exaggerated idealism leads ultimately to his rejection of the very terms of human existence — symbolized both by his suicide and by his mournful pronouncement to his former temptresses, Lucy and Isabel, just before it that "Pierre is neuter now!" (XXVI.vi.503).

The idealist in Conrad fares no better in his endeavor to make his life exemplary. Disregarding his innate limitations, he is driven by vanity to play a grandiose role out of keeping with his more modest talents. Morton Zabel's discussion of the central thematic concern in the early Conrad would seem of particular relevance to the author's skeptical regard for the idealist (and accounts as well for Melville's conception of the type):

> The conviction or delusion of a special destiny, an arbitrary assumption of superiority to common experience, a secret sense of the personal fate: it is these that possess his men, but invariably with a hint, covert or explicit, that this conviction will soon find itself at odds with the rough justice of fortune, the implacable or impersonal lines of life that disregard a man's idea of his own character or endowment and that will impose on him a test of reality for which youthful expectation, egotistic self-regard, or reckless self-law has little prepared him.[5]

Such an observation probably has its most pointed reference to Kurtz and Jim, two would-be benefactors of the human race whom events turn either into its contemptuous oppressor or its pitiful deserter. But it also has substantial applicability to such later characters as Charles Gould, Razumov, Heyst, and the Lingard of *The Rescue* — to say nothing of its pertinence to the careers of Taji, Ahab, and Pierre. The distaste for revolutionaries evident in

[5]"Introduction" to *Lord Jim*, p. xi.

Conrad's writing very likely can be viewed as deriving from this same wariness toward the individual whose vainglory blinded him to the truth about his capabilities and motives. Because any moral superiority man might assume could have no foundation other than egoism, it was intrinsically unsubstantial, unreliable, and, ultimately, unpraiseworthy. Melville, of course, could not repress a strong sympathy for the idealist — and doubtless this is one explanation of why Conrad disliked *Moby-Dick,* a work so lenient with its madly idealistic hero (as Conrad could never have been with Kurtz). Still, Melville is thorough enough in demonstrating the self-delusion of his visionaries. If he cannot finally censure them, it is for the same reason that Conrad's idealists, though sharply criticized, are left uncondemned. For the realists who oppose them, by lacking admirable ideals altogether, command far less sympathy — as do, for instance, the Reverend Mr. Falsgrave and Plotinus Plinlimmon in *Pierre*, the attorney in "Bartleby," and the Confidence Man; or, in Conrad, the white pilgrims in "Heart of Darkness," Sterne in "The End of the Tether," and Falk.

The essentially nonmoral drive for self-realization, which must be seen as accounting for the idealist's conduct, hints finally at the feebleness — even irrelevance — of objective moral categories. So long as man upheld his ideals only when they supplemented his basic needs, the codes adopted to judge man's behavior could be only accidentally related to the facts of experience. Such a state of affairs is perceived by Marlow in both "Heart of Darkness" and *Lord Jim*, and helps to define his moral anxiety. Likewise, Melville's heightened sense in *Pierre* of the ethical contradictions discernible in his hero's motives illuminates the impossible dilemma of the idealist position. It is a quandary made all the more bewildering by the realization that the notion of a "moral universe" is a myth and that, in consequence, all ethical principles must similarly be regarded as meaningless. Kurtz's "horror" has primarily to do with this consciousness that the irresponsible world into which man has been cast actually validates the stance of immorality. For if no rules can be detected in the general scheme of things, man might just as well abandon his socially approved principles of conduct and live according to his personal inclinations—however antisocial, even inhuman, they might be. Everything in the universe that remains "dark" to man's view, though not equivalent to what is evil (since its moral identity cannot be made out), nonetheless provides a basis for evil acts. As a result of this dangerous situation, the lucid man perceives that he may decide to act virtuously only in the face of facts that make such a decision unnecessarily restricting to his natural and (given the position of his lucidity) even justifiable impulse to exhaust life's possibilities.

The idealist, then, is capable neither of satisfactorily enacting his morally superior ideals, nor—to the extent that his sensitivity enables him to view these ideals objectively—of finding satisfactory warrant for them. His plight is suggested in *Victory* by Heyst's world-weary conclusion: "all action is bound to be harmful. It is devilish. That is why this world is evil upon the whole" (I.vi.54). But though this remark indicates the hero's awareness of how human involvement may intensify problems rather than mitigate them, and how it may encourage corruption rather than prevent it, the quietism that it implicitly advocates is demonstrated by the novel to be no less inadequate as a solution to man's dilemma. The choice of whether "to be or not to be" reduces itself to a choice between two negative alternatives when both responses are apt to lead to spiritual (if not physical) death. In Melville, the pacifist attitudes of Benito Cereno and Bartleby lead in the same unhappy direction as the activist positions of Taji, Ahab, and Pierre. And in Conrad, Heyst's pseudo solution of nonengagement to the problems raised by the involvement of a Kurtz or Jim is shown to be both untenable (Heyst himself must acknowledge that "it's difficult to resist where nothing matters" [*Victory*, III.iv.203]) and self-defeating. For unable to cut himself off from humanity altogether, Heyst is prompted to take on responsibility for the oppressed Lena; and unable to oppose Jones and his devilish accomplices actively, he sets into action the chain of circumstances that culminates in his self-destruction.

Just before his suicide, Heyst is moved to proclaim: "Woe to the man whose heart has not learned while young to hope, to love — and to put its trust in life!" (IV.xiv.410). And so we are made to see that even he — one of Conrad's most "informed" characters — has not so much been initiated into life through his nihilism as he has been initiated *out* of it. The sad consequence is that he is unprepared for his first profound experience with love, evil, suffering, and death — in short, with the vital components of human life. Left desolate by a reality that has overwhelmed him, he becomes at last skeptical about his skepticism and disenchanted with his disenchantment. And yet, even in spite of all this, the numerous instances of treachery in the novel expose the groundlessness of the trust that Heyst, reviewing the death that has been his life, is driven to promote. Considered in the total dramatic context, his cry seems more to express the book's general dilemma than to present a remedy for it. One of the traditional objections to *Victory* has been that the author's deepest vision is here compromised by a commitment to life almost sentimental in comparison; but it is questionable whether the book can be seen as glorifying life's possibilities. For its author remains at the same time skeptical about life and about the resistance to life.

The main point in *Victory* would appear to be that if man is to keep his humanity intact, he *must* retain his capacity for trust — and it is significant that in both Melville and Conrad the "villain" is the least trustful of characters. Also significant, however, is the fact that the villain, by making a career of betraying the hopes and beliefs of others, lends practical support to the contrary position of distrust. The problem, we see, is ultimately insoluble. It is important that one preserve some degree of faith in his fellow-men, and it is equally important that he realize the intrinsic dangers of this confidence. In *Israel Potter*, the fluent Benjamin Franklin would seem to offer a most sensible solution to the problem, but if we examine his words carefully, we recognize them as constituting, like Plinlimmon's lecture, an "excellently illustrated re-statement" of the dilemma rather than a solution to it. "An indiscriminate distrust of human nature," Franklin counsels the overly cautious Potter, now acting as secret messenger, "is the worst consequence of a miserable condition, whether brought about by innocence or guilt. And though want of suspicion more than want of sense, sometimes leads a man into harm, yet too much suspicion is as bad as too little sense" (vii.52). Franklin's recognition of the need to be discriminative about one's trust is, finally, platitudinous: his advice does not begin to handle the immensely difficult problem of deciding when a suspicious manner is warranted and when it is not. The adventures of Potter themselves are so shot through with incidents of betrayal and deception that in the end we must regard Franklin's eminently practical advice as, indeed, of no "practical" help at all. *The Confidence-Man*, which is the novel that succeeds *Israel Potter*, also exposes the attitude of trust as empirically unjustifiable. Exploring through its protean protagonist the infinitely varied types of betrayal, and presenting us with a world of unverifiable appearances, it reveals the foolishness of *not* being constantly on one's guard. As has already been noted, the confidence that prompts Don Benito to leave his slaves unchained is what leads to his fatal undoing.

The theme of betrayal is possibly even more widespread in Conrad's work, obliging us to view critically, at least from one angle, the author's well-known ideal of fidelity. For though faithfulness to some time-honored behavioral standard does have a kind of absolute value to it in Conrad's fiction, trusting in one's fellow-man is apt to end in misfortune or disaster, as is illustrated in the plots of such works as *An Outcast of the Islands*, "Karain," "The Lagoon," *Lord Jim* (i.e., Jim's trust in Gentleman Brown), "Amy Foster," *Nostromo, The Secret Agent,* and *Under Western Eyes.*

In a world where so little can be ascertained — where treachery and trustworthiness are inseparably mixed, where man's own motives are never wholly decipherable, and where the world outside man must remain an enigma — there can be no set response to the problem of "how to be." The ideals that Melville and Conrad most admire—integrity, fidelity, trust, charity, solidarity—are neither objectively commendable nor, generally, even personally prudent. The oracular Stein in *Lord Jim* might at first appear to offer a workable strategy for the problem, but upon inspection his advice on "following the dream" hardly can be understood as providing us with a definite solution.

In what is probably the most frequently quoted passage in the novel, Stein remarks to Marlow:

> "A man that is born falls into a dream like a man into the sea. If he tries to climb out into the air as inexperienced people endeavour to do, he drowns—*nicht wahr?* . . .No! I tell you! The way is to the destructive element submit yourself, and with the exertions of your hands and feet in the water make the deep, deep sea keep you up. So if you ask me—how to be?. . .That was the way. To follow the dream, and again to follow the dream— and so—*ewig—usque ad finem.* . . ." (xx.214-215)

Usually these lines are inferred as criticism of Jim's "airy" romanticism, of either his quixotic tendencies or his cowardly evasions of reality. But we have already called attention to Marlow's doubt over whether Jim's choice to live and rule in Patusan "amounted to shirking his ghost or to facing him out"—whether, that is, his retreat to a remote spot on earth was "flight" or actually "a mode of combat" (xix.197). We cannot be certain that Jim has managed to immerse himself in the destructive element, or, on the contrary, that he has contrived to avoid it. Stein's own comment on the youth: "He is romantic—romantic. . . . And that is very bad—very bad. . . . Very good, too" (xx.216), represents no less equivocal an evaluation of Jim. His comment would even seem indirectly to suggest some ambivalence about his own "romantic" mode of life. "To follow the dream"—or perhaps more accurately, to follow *one's* dream—as is characteristic of the romantic, assures neither personal success nor failure.

Of all the commentary on Stein's apparently judicious pronouncement, that of Albert Guerard seems, in its reservations about accepting Stein as Conrad's final spokesman, one of the most sensible. To Guerard, Stein's obvious integrity combined with "the memorably cryptic quality of his utterance" dispose us to place our confidence in his judgment and identify it with Conrad's. But the cogency of Stein's idea that man must actively engage himself in order to make viable his illusions of self (a reading opposed, Guerard points out, to the common one that "man must learn to live with his unideal limitations") is nevertheless undermined by the imagery following his advice. As Guerard notes, this imagery "associates Stein and his 'conviction' with the half-lights of deception and menacing illusion; it brings Stein down to Jim's level rather than raises Jim to his. We cannot be sure what Conrad thought about Stein. Neither, possibly, could Conrad himself."[6] In consequence, although we may be inclined to acknowledge Stein's success in following his own dream, in meaningfully combining thought and action, his enigmatic expression furnishes us, finally, with little authoritative counsel on the question of how best to conduct one's existence. Indeed, the fact that his lines have been so variously interpreted by the critics suggests that his advice *is* finally ambiguous and therefore incapable of resolving the dilemma it so impressively tackles.

Absorbed in everyday routine, most people are never obliged to come to direct terms with the most crucial problems of existence. Instinctively shunning the "issue" of meaningful behavior, they conveniently adhere to their conventional notions of right and wrong as though it were impossible for them to give way under pressure. In the fiction of Melville and Conrad, however, situations have a way of compelling man to take fully into account those things that most men, with their uncanny instinct for survival, dare not even consider. The result of such reckoning can often be fatal, and the frequency of man's taking his own life in the two authors is scarcely coincidental. In Melville, the consciousness of one's dilemma almost invariably leads to some form of suicide, as evidenced

[6]*Conrad the Novelist*, p. 164. See also pp. 165-166.

in the fates of Taji, Ahab, Pierre, Bartleby, and Benito Cereno. In Conrad, the number of those who take their lives is also inordinately high and includes such characters as Kayerts, Captain Brierly, Captain Whalley, Decoud, Winnie Verloc, Renouard, de Barral, and Heyst—not to mention such borderline cases as Jim, Flora de Barral, Razumov, and Peyrol.

It is possible, of course, to understand all these suicides as fictional sublimations of the two authors' recurrent impulse to escape from their own stressful lives. In addition, the self-destructive motives of honor or lost love in Conrad's fiction may be plausibly related to circumstances in the author's life that may well have left him with an overwhelming sense of guilt or despair. Conrad's own youthful attempt at suicide in Marseilles suggests the most spectacular cause for his preoccupation with people killing themselves. Beneath these popular explanations for the prevalence of suicides in Conrad specifically, we may recognize as the key factor a spiritual disillusionment akin to that which plagues Melville's death-seekers. Obliged to confront moral chaos as well as their own helplessness in coping with it, they are tempted toward complete withdrawal. Without the spiritual stamina to throw themselves back into life's masquerade, they choose the stasis of non-life. As Marlow remarks in *Chance*: "Suicide, I suspect, is very often the outcome of mere mental weariness—not an act of savage energy but the final symptom of complete collapse" (I.vi.183). Such a reflection serves as commentary not only on such characters as Captain Brierly, Captain Whalley, Decoud, Winnie Verloc, Renouard, and Heyst, but also on such Melville suicides as Pierre, Bartleby, and Benito Cereno. The terrific strain of having to face the bombardment of one's most sustaining ideals—as Don Benito must face the brutality of "the Negro" and Captain Brierly the unaccountable dishonor of a Jim—leads to a despondency that can find relief only in the annihilation of self.

The predicament of living reasonably in a world perceived as reasonless is one that, outside of the demonic Confidence Man and—with a few reservations—Conrad's Stein, no major character in the two authors is able to solve. If there is, indeed, some practical way of surviving the disabling shock of life's horrors, it could hardly be based on essential truth. For both authors were driven to confess that such truth was ultimately nihilistic and nullified formulas of conduct altogether. All that is left, then, is (to use Marlow's term) the truth of "surface reality," and it will be seen that the positive values both authors promote in their fiction are not arrived at logically so much as morally. They are advanced not because they are justifiable, but—more important—because they are felt to be absolutely necessary.

Though flimsy illusion may at first seem unpromising ground for the growth of ideals, it is at least more hospitable than the soil of objective truth. Melville and Conrad may have been determined truth-seekers, but neither was disposed to forsake his moral ideals because his sallies after truth exposed their tenuousness, at times even their untenability. As Melville has his title character finally exclaim in *Clarel*, that soberly affirmative poem of his old age,

> "Conviction is not gone
> Though faith's gone: that which shall not be
> Still *ought* to be!" (IV.xxx.285)

In insisting upon the necessity of certain ideals, both writers rejected, if not the logic of their negative line of thought, at least its ultimate human worth. Much better in the end, they realized, for one to act well under illusion than dubiously under truth.

Melville never elects actually to speak out in behalf of illusions, but his frequent illustrations of truth's undermining nature suggest his awareness of their value. Conrad, however, asserts throughout his fictional career the worth-while nature of illusions, regardless of how self-deceptive they may be. In the preface to *Almayer's Folly*, he writes of "the curse of facts and the blessing of illusions" (p. x), and in his early story "The Return" he points out the desperate need for shelter against life's distressing truths. For once a person has

endured the climactic moment of lucidity: "there is a moment of
dumb dismay, and the wanderings must begin again; the painful
explaining away of facts, the feverish raking up of illusions, the
cultivation of a fresh crop of lies in the sweat of one's brow, to
sustain life, to make it supportable, to make it fair. . ." (*Tales of
Unrest*, p. 134). If one cannot "rake up" new illusions to compen-
sate for those lost, he is destined to suffer the plight of a Benito
Cereno, Bartleby, Captain Brierly, Decoud—or, indeed, of an Alvan
Hervey, the melodramatic and egotistical hero of "The Return"
whose disillusioning knowledge about his wife's short affair ini-
tiates him step by step into life's absurdity and at last prompts
him literally to walk out on his entire life. His mental examination
of the "dishonouring episode" (p. 160) reminds us of Marlow's
description of the overwrought Captain Brierly, whose dangerous
identification with Jim "start[s] into life some thought with which a
man unused to such companionship finds it impossible to live"
(vi.59).

Marlow, like his creator, realizes that the perception of life's
incongruities is to be feared, since it inevitably weakens one's feeling of well-being. Contrasting the value of an unthinking faith to
a ruminative commitment to facts, he must conclude: "Hang ideas!
They are tramps, vagabonds, knocking at the back-door of your
mind, each taking a little of your substance, each carrying away
some crumb of that belief in a few simple notions you must cling to
if you want to live decently and would like to die easy!" (*LJ*, v.43).
In such a passage we may glimpse Conrad's dilemma as man and
artist: motivated at once by the desire to pursue general truths
and to uphold ethical standards, he is at one point compelled to
acknowledge the contradiction between his metaphysical and moral
ideals. Since truth's cost is exorbitant in terms of the sweet and
consoling illusions that must be given up for it, Conrad had finally
to relent in a quest hostile to one's peace of mind. Though he may
himself be willing to hold a lantern up to life's darkness, he is too
socially committed an artist to explore the unorthodox ethical implications of his scrutiny. For as he tells us in *Victory:* "every age is

fed on illusions, lest men should renounce life early and the human race come to an end" (II.iii.94).

Besides seeing illusions as vital to the continuation of mankind, Conrad also regarded them as essential in helping the individual to escape the paralysis of thought that kept him from living productively. Once again, we find in *Victory* Conrad's most forceful support for a viewpoint uninformed of life's vacuum. Writing of Heyst's upbringing, Conrad observes: "The young man learned to reflect, which is a destructive process, a reckoning of the cost. It is not the clear-sighted who lead the world. Great achievements are accomplished in a blessed, warm mental fog, which the pitiless cold blasts of the father's analysis had blown away from the son" (II.iii.91-92). The author's tone here may be undeniably ironic, but there is nothing ironic about his thought: truth is chilling and stultifies all effort; vague, insubstantial belief (as long as it is not recognized as such) is reassuring and promotes worthwhile endeavors. Although Heyst's blanket generalization that "all action is bound to be harmful" is not without a sort of perverse validity, it represents nonetheless a completely negative attitude toward life and can result only in the suicidal passivity of a Bartleby or the practical paralysis of a Decoud—who, near his end, is convinced of the "utter uselessness of all effort" (*Nostromo*, III.x.500). On the other hand, we have the dim-witted Captains Delano and Mitchell, whose stubborn faith in their security enables them to act in such a way that their welfare can survive all that threatens it. Their illusions help them emerge victorious in situations that could not but defeat the two authors' more sensitive characters.

However unreasonable illusions may be, then, Conrad might yet maintain a reasoned belief in their value. Moral ideals themselves may be only illusory, but that hardly renders a belief in them inane; and Conrad is able to pay genuine tribute to certain values while fully aware that they admit of no absolute sanction. For the important thing is that these values are indispensable in making human existence nobler and more estimable than the primitive animal life destined to prevail in their absence. Man's adherence to ideals of honor and duty may seem arbitrary in a meaningless universe, but such fidelity all the same affirms his capacity to transcend ethically the amoral world around him and claims our respect. Conrad's enduring belief in the value of social commitments may in fact remind us of contemporary existential thinkers who, after acknowledging life's natural insignificance, go on to postulate ethical standards they feel deserve man's deepest consideration. Perhaps the greatest paradox in Conrad's work is that it simultaneously discloses the ultimate irrelevance of moral ideals and provides eloquent—and *morally* meaningful—arguments for their acceptance. Despite his intrepid skepticism, his insistence on the worth of traditional ethical codes makes his fiction a predominantly moral one. In this regard—it deserves to be emphasized—he does not strike us as especially related to Melville, whose imagination tended to focus as much on irresoluble metaphysical questions as on matters of ethical conduct. Still, it should be evident that Melville's dramas, in exposing the inadequacy of certain exceptional patterns of behavior, are very similar to Conrad's in moral implication.

The defeat of the isolated or independent man is a common theme in both their works and indicates the need for that solidarity which Conrad frequently advanced as man's greatest resource against an alien universe—as well as against his own perilous egoism. By choosing to insulate himself from the human community, one chose a way of life full of dangers and almost devoid of rewards. In *Under Western Eyes*, Razumov proclaims: "I am independent—and therefore perdition is my lot" (IV.iv.362); and the hazards involved in a determined individuality are demonstrated again and again in the two authors. The over-reliance upon self results in the severing of one's most vital bonds to society and a consequent inability to act purposefully. The independence of an Ahab, Pierre, or Bartleby, or of a Kurtz, Razumov, or Heyst, leads neither to private contentment nor public constructiveness. Exiled by his refusal to share man's common fate, the "isolato" suffers both morally and spiritually. If he gains the freedom he has craved, this same freedom ultimately prompts him toward conduct beneficial neither to himself nor society.

Further, the terrible loneliness of the isolated self may lead to insanity or suicide. We might, for instance, accurately account for Kurtz's moral madness in Africa by stressing "the intense concentration of self in the middle of such heartless immensity," noting at the same time that this Conradian description is not Conrad's at all but Melville's used to portray the sad fate of the castaway Pip in *Moby-Dick*, who is left by Stubb to sink or swim in the "awful lonesomeness" of the ocean (II.xciii.169). In both cases, having to cope alone with the overwhelming and anarchic forces of nature ends in mental collapse. Decoud is another figure of abandonment and suffers a fate even more drastic. Compelled to live in utter solitude for eleven enfeebling days on the Golfo Placido, he finally breaks down, losing all assured sense of his place in the overall scheme of things. If he escapes insanity—and in *Under Western Eyes* Conrad declares that "no human being could bear a steady view of moral solitude without going mad" (I.ii.39)—it is only because he drowns himself beforehand. Having to relinquish all of man's life-saving illusions, he is destined, as the author tells us, to be "swallowed up in the immense indifference of things" (*Nostromo*, III.x.501).

In order to elude the horrifying sense of nature's indifference, man must maintain a belief in human devotion. As Conrad wrote in *A Personal Record*: "the world, the temporal world, rests on a few very simple ideas [meaning here, frankly, "illusions"]; so simple that they must be as old as the hills. It rests notably, among others, on the idea of Fidelity" (p.xxi). Even so, the thematic structure of Conrad's fiction exhibits a constant tension between man's irremediable loneliness and his capacity for love and fellowship—a tension discernible in Melville's work as well. And while the narrators Ishmael and Marlow may speak out regularly for the cause of human brotherhood, they themselves can never quench their feelings of isolation. Indeed, Ishmael's very name is a synonym for the social outcast. Endowed with a sharp sense of moral responsibility, however, both narrators are constrained to advocate what will always be slightly beyond them. When Conrad in his preface to *The Nigger of the "Narcissus"* wrote of the artist's appealing to our "invincible conviction of solidarity that knits together the loneliness of innumerable hearts" (p. xii), he intimated his limited faith in fellowship by implying that what solidarity actually does is not to eradicate individual loneliness but to make a kind of larger human unity out of it. Loneliness, his words suggest, may be "shared" and thereby alleviated, but can hardly be discarded as an animal might shed an outer layer of skin. Because Conrad, and Melville also, are fundamentally solitaries themselves, the paramount value they impute to fellowship strikes us as assigned more out of desperation than faith. Like all other humanly fabricated ideals, it can be grounded only in illusion since man *is* essentially a lonely being destined, as Marlow says in "Heart of Dearkness," to live and dream uncommunicating and alone. Still, neither author was inclined to expose the meager foundation of brotherhood: the harsh reality of man's isolation was by itself intolerable, and it was therefore imperative that a belief in solidarity be clung to as a viable remedy for it.

When in *Nostromo* we are informed that the cause of Decoud's death is "solitude and want of faith in himself and others" (III.x.496), it is evident that the author is indirectly invoking the necessity of a deeply felt commitment toward self and society. Without this commitment, one's consciousness — and conscience — is in continual peril of being snatched away by the currents of nihilism. In the absence of stabilizing human ties, one may at any time be sucked under by the awareness of emptiness. Decoud, in his irresponsibly "erect[ing] passions into duties" (III.x.498), cannot survive in his crisis the despair that comes of perceiving one's miserable vacancy. Spiritually estranged from humanity, he loses the crucial ability to counter the vicissitudes of fortune. The same is true of Heyst, who, also lacking faith in life and in his fellow-man, pridefully removes himself from the human enterprise. Convinced that "he who forms a tie is lost [since] the germ of corruption has entered into his soul" (*Victory*, III.iii.199-200), he prefers to keep himself safely aloof in his ivory tower. But his stubborn refusal to recognize the tangible ideals of love and fellowship and to fulfill their commitments renders him virtually helpless before the evil presence of Jones.

In Melville, too, the person who allows his private values to override all other considerations is eventually defeated by the world he has renounced. Either rebelling against his social obligations or cutting himself off from them, he forsakes his chances of earthly salvation and condemns himself to a life of discontent and unhappiness. Taji, Ahab, Pierre, and Bartleby may have their own special reasons for acting as they do, but basically they all "prefer not to" participate in the common human fate; and such preference operates to make them all, in the end, merely the "fools of fate." Though both Melville and Conrad repeatedly admit the difficulties of acting wisely, and generally refrain from offering specific recommendations of their own, they show throughout their careers a deep respect for social relationships capable of nourishing the individual and society. Melville, it might be mentioned, gives particular stress to the value of fraternity, and the picture of two men living together and helping each other is a familiar one in his work: we find in such a relationship Tommo and Toby, Omoo and Doctor Long Ghost, Taji and Jarl, Redburn and Harry Bolton, White Jacket and Jack Chase, and—most notably—Ishmael and Queequeg.

"Woe to the straggler!" Marlow exclaims in *Lord Jim*. "We exist only in so far as we hang together" (xxi.223). Only by acting so as to fulfill his duty to his fellow-men can one experience the feeling of significance crucial to well-being. In *Mardi*, it is the land of Serenia—where spiritual love prevails and all men respond to each other as brothers—that is finally presented as offering man relief from his egocentric and endlessly frustrated quest for an absolute and "unholy" satisfaction in life. Moreover, man achieves his mortal destiny most fully not by making the claims of society subservient to his private impulses but by the reverse. In return, cooperative action gives one's life the meaning—or more accurately, the *illusion* of meaning—that he requires if he is to feel his identity distinct from the amorphous world around him. For left wholly to himself, he must eventually be demoralized by the sense of his own internal chaos. Generalizing on Decoud's fate in *Nostromo*, Conrad points out that "in our activity alone do we find the sustaining illusion of an independent existence as against the whole scheme of things of which we form a helpless part" (III.x.497).

Because society cannot rescue man from the alien universe or from himself unless it is capable of maintaining objective standards, both authors recognized that at times personal rights—even individual justice—had to be sacrificed so that the social system might remain secure. Such a consideration of social expediency accounts for Captain Vere's determination to execute the fundamentally innocent Budd—a socially responsible (if unmerciful) decision to which Melville may have felt bound to acquiesce. For the anarchic situation that leniency toward the unquestionable murderer of Claggart might precipitate had to be avoided at all costs. And in the end, it was more merciful to harden one's heart against his compassion and withstand the natural appeal of a virtuous man's case than to jeopardize the social order essential for the general good. In placing a higher value on the preservation of the imperfect community than on the "perfect" individual, Captain Vere paradoxically affirms his common humanity in the very suspension of it. Conrad's heroic Captains—most notably Captain Beard in "Youth," Captain Allistoun in *The Nigger*, and Captain MacWhirr in *Typhoon*—all resemble Vere in seeing the welfare of the ship (an obvious emblem or microcosm of society) as a more important consideration than the well-being of any of its crew. And in each tale the duty of man is shown to be the subordination of his will to the will of the ship. By subduing his egoism in this way, he may succeed in accomplishing his small part in protecting the social order, which, in turn, could continue to protect him.

When, on the other hand, the dictates of social morality are subordinated to private ambition, the results are not only socially destructive but self-destructive as well. Playing life's intricate game according to one's own rules only multiplies its difficulties. In *Pierre*, Melville warns of the outcome of an insistent adherence to one's freedom by noting the "perils and the miseries" attendant upon his hero's obstinate disregard for society's code in his pursuit of Isabel's cause. For in disdaining "those arbitrary lines of conduct, by which the common world, however base and dastardly, surrounds [him] for [his] worldly good" (X.i.246), Pierre gives up the very supports that he, like everybody else, needs to live a personally gratifying life. Made more vulnerable to the lawless instincts of the unbridled psyche, Pierre must continually fight for control of his ethical self with an ever-weakening belief in its objective reality. Having abandoned faith in society's sovereign authority, he must eventually lose faith in all else and become the hapless victim of his antisocial, though initially noble, plan of action.

The individual idealism of a Kurtz also becomes corrupted in the absence of all recognized authority. And in this case the moral deterioration is doomed to be more extreme, since Kurtz's primeval surroundings and his own assumed dominion over the natives give an almost boundless freedom to his instinctive anarchic impulses. Marlow's explanation for his subject's fearful diabolism makes clear the ethical value of society's "arbitrary lines of conduct." Keeping the ignorance of his auditors in mind, he ruefully observes: "He had taken a high seat amongst the devils of the land. . . . How can you imagine what particular region of the first ages a man's untrammelled feet may take him into by the way of solitude—utter solitude without a policeman—by the way of silence—utter silence, where no warning voice of a kind neighbour can be heard whispering of public opinion. These little things make all the great difference" (*Youth*, ii.116). When Kurtz breaks his links with civilized society in his no longer controllable will to power, he ceases to exist within the human context. As Marlow puts it later on: "There was nothing either above or below him. . . . He had kicked himself loose of the earth. Confound the man! he had kicked the very earth to pieces" (iii.144). Transgressing, like Ahab, the limits of his jurisdiction, he does violence both to himself and to the world about him.

All this is hardly to say that Melville and Conrad believed that following the rules of one's culture would enable a person to live happily ever after. While the two authors may have been convinced that adhering to the traditional regulations and restraints set up by society was the only effective way to cope with life's problems, neither was so optimistic as to feel that such devotion guaranteed personal contentment. In safeguarding the general welfare, society was not really fit to cooperate with anyone's individual needs. And in addition, the world beyond society was naturally hostile to many of man's desires. In both authors, therefore, we find abundant evidence that the attitude of stoical resignation is itself to be regarded as an important human value. In Melville, the fruitlessness of revolting against society and the human condition—as exemplified most notably by Taji, Ahab, Pierre, and Bartleby—is made depressingly clear. And so if one is to derive any satisfaction at all from life, he must learn to make the best of its unchangeable inequities, a "lesson" that forms the key point of such stories as "The Fiddler" and "Jimmy Rose." As Ishmael wisely, and acquiescently, reflects:

> Who ain't a slave? Tell me that. When, then, however the old sea-captains may order me about—however they may thump and punch me about, I have the satisfaction of knowing that it is all right; that everybody else is one way or other served in much the same way—either in a physical or metaphysical point of view, that is; and so the universal thump is passed around, and all hands should rub each other's shoulder-blades, and be content. (M-D, I.i.5)

Ishmael's solution—or better, salve—to what is ultimately beyond cure is for men to cooperatively "rub each other's shoulder-blades"; and it is Conrad's suggested remedy also. For the central value of solidarity so noticeable in Conrad's work originates out of the author's awareness of cosmic and social injustices, which, though they cannot be gotten rid of, can at least be palliated by the balm of brotherhood and mutual understanding. By himself, man cannot for long endure "the universal thump," but if he can somehow manage to *share* his pain with his fellow sufferers, he may profitably make use of most of the worldly comforts extended to him. And in his undying capacity to find means of consolation for the everlasting pang of being human, he may discover a personally rewarding way of affirming that destiny which, in the end, it is only suicidal to protest.

CHAPTER VI

MELVILLE AND CONRAD'S MODERNITY

Neither Melville's fiction nor Conrad's is characteristic of its age. The movement toward literary realism dominant in their times could hardly be expected to attract two writers less interested in mirroring surface reality than in penetrating to murky subterranean regions. The verisimilitude so many of their contemporaries strove for could not but appear inadequate and unsatisfactory to them.

Melville accounts for his opposition to the realistic novelist of the day most pointedly in *The Confidence-Man,* where in a chapter of Fieldingesque commentary he takes up the matter of true and false depiction of character. Freely admitting that he has treated one of his characters inharmoniously, he defends himself by arguing that "in real life a consistent character is a *rara avis*" (xiv.89). To Melville, reality is approached not by regularizing human actions but by presenting them in their most contradictory and confounding aspects. Criticizing the novelist more loyal to his artistic formulas for the different human types than to the far less easily identifiable counterparts of these types in actuality, he comments: "That fiction, where every character can, by reason of its consistency, be comprehended at a glance, either exhibits but sections of character, making them appear for wholes, or else is very untrue to reality; while, on the other hand, that author who draws a character, even though to common view incongruous in its parts. . .may yet, in so doing, be not false but faithful to the facts" (xiv.90). By refusing to conform to the conventional expectations of what a novelist ought and ought not to do, Melville denied the validity of the prevalent literary standards of his time. As Willard Thorp has stated (though with some exaggeration): "his conception of what constituted reality in fiction was utterly at variance with the dominant attitude of the mid-century, which had yet to be given the name realism, though it had manifested itself abundantly in art and literature and was already accepted as a fixed critical canon."[1]

Conrad, too, felt that the artist could not reach reality by working within the framework of conventional realism, and he once counseled Arnold Bennett to divorce himself from his rigidly realistic commitments so that he might be less handicapped in discovering the inner meanings of his subject matter. "You stop just short of being absolutely real," he wrote Bennett, "because you are faithful to your dogmas of realism. Now realism in art will never approach reality."[2] To Conrad, the creed of objective realism was not so much a way of coping with life's incongruities as it was a means of pushing them into the background. In a largely literal transcription of the common facts of life, the artist, he felt, shunned his foremost responsibility of breathing meaningful life into his raw materials. When Conrad wrote that "the road to legitimate realism is through poetical feeling" (*Notes on Life and Letters*, p. 56), he suggested that until a novelist was able to grasp imaginatively the experience he wished to convey, he could not succeed in doing it full justice.

We have already discussed Melville and Conrad's predisposition toward the limited narrative perspective, a technical preference that should indicate their distrust of the objectivist assumptions of the realistic school of writing. For the realists believed that reality was obtainable through a systematic and dispassionate recording of it, whereas Melville and Conrad felt that such reproduction was ultimately as false to reality as it was immediately true to it. If a work of fiction were to be truly suggestive of the human situation,

---

[1] "Introduction" to *Herman Melville: Representative Selections* (New York, 1938), p. xliv.

[2] 10 March 1902, in *Life and Letters*, I, 303.

the author had, they believed, not only to dramatize experience coherently and convincingly, but also to relate how that experience was *felt* by the person involved. They saw the attempt to objectify life by depersonalizing it as falsifying the way life offered itself to man. Since whatever meaning an event had was located in (and limited by) the subject's response to it, both authors recognized the need of a fictional form that resolutely confined itself to the narrow boundaries of the subjective. Because of this subjectivism, we are not permitted to understand a Bartleby any more adequately than does the attorney; or to appreciate a Kurtz or Jim any better than does a Marlow. However, in our being presented with a vivid *impression* of these characters, we may gain a better sense of them than would be possible through a more objective account.

Both writers, aware that the final truth of events was relative, naturally rebelled against a literary movement based on the conviction that reality was best approached by disinterested "reporting" (as if the court depositions of a Benito Cereno could, if exhaustive enough, yield the essential truth of that man's encounter). In short, both authors rejected contemporary notions of realism as insufficiently realistic. Their own more impressionistic undertakings struck them as much more capable of reflecting the truth embedded in experience.

Although it may appear contradictory at this point to say so, if Melville and Conrad were essentially more "realistic" than the realists, they were at the same time more romantic as well. For rather than concentrate on the ordinary facets of life, they chose instead to focus on characters and situations clearly exceptional in nature. What intrigued them was not so much common humanity as uncommon heroism—regardless of how debased that heroism might eventually turn out to be. Whether Ahab and Kurtz, for example, are finally more deserving of blame than of praise in no way affects their extraordinary stature as human specimens; and their strenuous efforts to master what must inevitably master them serves to link them much more closely to the romantic figures of the past than to the more life-size heroes of their contemporaries.

The attraction that the unusual and adventurous held for both writers even accounts for the superficial resemblances of some of their narratives to the adolescent tale of adventure.

But however romantic Melville and Conrad may have been in their construction of plot and character, they were rarely disposed to treat their materials with anything like romantic abandon, for their understanding of man's egoism disinclined them from idealizing any of his pursuits. Much too skeptical to accept his motives at face value, they both demonstrated in their fiction a profound disbelief in man's noble capacities. In *White Jacket*, Melville tells his reader quite plainly that although he is gravely concerned about the abuses that sailors are made to endure in an American warship, he is under no "literary" illusions about the character of these seamen. As he puts it: "Be it here, once and for all, understood, that no sentimental and theoretic love for the common sailor; no romantic belief in that peculiar noble-heartedness and exaggerated generosity of disposition fictitiously imputed to him in novels. . .have actuated me in anything I have said. . ." (lxxii.381). Having had the opportunity to know sailors firsthand, Melville must emphasize that their traditional glorification is a flagrant misrepresentation of the facts. Committed in his own writing to honest evaluation of the real world, he is never in much danger of being "taken in" by the play of his imagination, however erratic his choice of scenes and characters may sometimes be.

Conrad, too, although he may be drawn to the spectacular rather than the ordinary, manages to avoid glorifying his subjects. A romantic at heart, his mental perspective is yet that of a severe realist. As he once wrote: "the romantic feeling of reality was in me an inborn faculty. This in itself may be a curse but when disciplined by a sense of personal responsibility and a recognition of the hard facts of existence shared with the rest of mankind becomes but a point of view from which the very shadows of life appear endowed with an internal glow. And such romanticism is not a sin" (*Within the Tides*, pp. vii-viii). The use of character doubling in Conrad (and, to a lesser extent, in Melville also) may be seen as but one way that the romantic protagonist is presented to us in line with "the hard facts of existence." For though Conrad might seem romantic in his occasional tendency to divide his characters into moral categories, he nevertheless contrives to make them lifelike by furnishing them with alter egos to mirror their contrary potentialities. Through the technique of doubling, what originally appeared to be white turns out to be one of various shades of gray. Heyst, for example, may seem ethically superior to the corrupt world in which he exists, but the many traits he shares with the unscrupulous Jones make us all too conscious of his own morally mixed nature. And even in Melville, the morality of Ahab's glorious goal of slaying the leviathan to free man from the world's evil is made deeply suspect by the author's studied employment of the demonic Fedallah to serve as his second self.

Melville and Conrad's faithfulness to reality is also evidenced by the close adherence of their fiction either to personal experience or to actual happenings of their time. Distrusting the unbridled imagination, both were disposed to base their narrative on a solid core of fact; and a number of their works are so deeply rooted in autobiography that it seems almost illegitimate to apply the conventional standards of prose fiction to them. If critics (as opposed to biographers) have had comparatively little to say about such Melville works as *Typee, Omoo, Redburn,* and *White Jacket,* it is because their basic designs have almost as much to do with the fluctuations of life as with the forms of art. Melville may at various points have "heightened" facts and even invented new episodes, but his ambition to communicate intact his private experiences and his reflections over them make these books as much fact as fiction. Even in such an unquestionably artistic creation as *Moby-Dick,* the imaginative and rhetorical flights are tempered by a constant recourse to fact and autobiographical remembrance. Linking the romantic-realistic novel to its predecessors, Charles Feidelson has described its method as generally the "fictional enhancement of [Melville's] actual experiences."[3]

[3]"Introduction" to *Moby-Dick* (Indianapolis, 1964), p. xv.

The substantial autobiographical element in many of Conrad's tales is perhaps even more striking, and, as we might expect, critics have regularly called attention to it. Indeed, Conrad himself frequently confessed his deep indebtedness to personal experience in giving body to his writing. Like Melville, he tended to trust in the situations and events of his life to keep his romantic faculty from getting the better of his judgment and misdirecting his attempts to get at the underlying meanings of reality. Even such an imaginative triumph as "Heart of Darkness" owes more to the author's considerable powers of recollection than it does to any special inventiveness. Though the tale may not be as straightforwardly autobiographical as "Youth" or *The Shadow Line,* its essential authenticity is easily verified by an inspection of the diary kept by Conrad during his Congo journey. And the author freely acknowledged the tale's source in reality by speaking of it as "experience pushed a little (and only a little) beyond the actual facts of the case"—going on to justify this "fictional enhancement" by telling us that it was for "the perfectly legitimate. . .purpose of bringing [the experience] home to the minds and bosoms of the readers" (*Youth,* p. xi).

One other way that Melville and Conrad strove to make their narratives undistorted reflections of the real world was to inject into them a multitude of lifelike particulars. Anxiously concerned with achieving verisimilitude, they occasionally even risked boring the reader with an abundance of details. For if they were to demonstrate successfully the validity of their viewpoint, they sensed the necessity of first convincing the reader that the universe before him lacked nothing in credibility and was, therefore, worthy of his sustained trust. Only through a dense "documentation" of their tales did they believe they could accomplish their primary function as artists, a function Conrad defined with admirable brevity in the preface to *The Nigger of the "Narcissus."* Feeling that art could activate its audience only by making a specific impression on its senses, Conrad confided that his own most cherished ambition as writer was "by the power of the written word to make you hear, to make you feel. . .[and] before all, to make you *see"* (p. xiv).

Ultimately, of course, making us see meant making us *understand*, and both authors realized that the deeper significations of a thing became accessible only by first creating an overall "feel" for its surface presence. Intuitively, the two writers put their artistic faith in the familiar adage "seeing is believing" and endeavored to provide us with maximum exposure to their created worlds so that we might better perceive their underlying truths. One of the greatest defects of *Mardi* is that in it Melville abandoned his concern for verisimilitude in his irrepressible urge toward metaphysical speculation, thereby losing hold on the reality he needed to make his story compelling to the reader. Realizing his critical error, he took every opportunity in *Moby-Dick,* his next sally into the thin air of the imaginative, to place the phantomlike whale and his quasi-mythical pursuer within a context whose realistic specificities would insure the reader's abiding belief. Milton Stern's comment on *Moby-Dick* should help suggest the fruitful mixture of romanticism and realism not only in Melville's greatest works but in Conrad's as well. "Melville used fact," he points out, "to provide a basis for a naturalistic perception that he expresses romantically, poetically, and symbolically."[4]

By using material reality to maintain contact with the actual world, both authors felt that their art might then justifiably extend its meanings. Conrad suggested as much when he wrote to a friend: ". . .I don't start with an abstract notion. I start with definite images and as their rendering is true some little effect is produced."[5] By concentrating upon the reality of his concretions, Conrad trusted them to take on symbolic dimensions in the natural course of exposition without any manipulation on his part. If he were painstakingly honest about them and withstood the temptation of affixing to them any certain significations, they might attain proportions broader than their literal selves. Melville, too, sought to establish solid grounds for suggestive meanings by attending to images in

[4]"Some Techniques of Melville's Perception," p. 121n.

[5]Letter to R. B. Cunninghame Graham, 8 February 1899, in *Life and Letters,* I, 268.

such a way that they might become imbued with symbolic import. Babo, for example, is evocative of moral blackness not because he is handled mythically (as Melville had earlier handled Yillah in *Mardi*), nor because he is explicitly interpreted for us as such, but because we are made to *see* him so vividly that we are compelled to "read" him on a higher level of abstraction in order to make sense of his actions.

Not always, however, could Melville and Conrad let things speak for themselves. In *Moby-Dick* and "Heart of Darkness" particularly, they employed symbolizing narrators who might say within an artistic context what they as authors were forbidden to say from without. Both Ishmael and Marlow are intrigued by sensory reality and delight in elaborate descriptions of it, but neither is satisfied with a merely "pictorial" presentation of his experience. Needing to locate some strand of significance in all that appears alien to the self, the two narrators attempt to assimilate each new contact into a unified and coherent vision of reality—which itself is perpetually in flux since it must be modified by each new object of perception. On another level, both narrators urgently quest after meaningful symbols so that they will not be overwhelmed by the chaos of reality—as, for example, is Kurtz. Ishmael can help protect himself against the dangerous sea by reflecting upon its inherent treacherousness. And Marlow can resist the jungle's primitive appeal to his own repressed savagery by articulating to himself the threat it poses: by analyzing what is symbolized by the wilderness he may decrease his vulnerability to it.

What is psychologically and practically beneficial about symbolizing to Ishmael and Marlow is at the same time artistically valuable, for it allows the narration to achieve a depth unattainable through direct naturalistic description. We may recall Marlow's famous exclamation on rivets, the item he desperately requires in order to mend his steamboat and begin his journey to the Inner Station. As actual metal bolts these rivets are precious enough, of course, but when Marlow goes on to enlarge upon their utility by informing us that "rivets were what really Mr. Kurtz wanted, if he had only known it" (*Youth*, i.84), we see their symbolic import as well. They are what man needs to keep things stable and secure, and, by further implication, what he requires to act disinterestedly and with purpose. The application of Marlow's symbolic imagination to rivets vividly suggests the materialistic base for the larger meanings we find elsewhere in "Heart of Darkness" and throughout *Moby-Dick*. Symbols are not intuited in any transcendentalist fashion from natural forms but derived empirically—and always tentatively—from the contemplation of factual data.

If the best works of Melville and Conrad are, finally, more appropriately seen as symbolic than realistic, it is because the central interest of both authors is not so much with actuality as with all the meanings that might legitimately be inferred from it. Two critical quotations, the first pertaining to Melville, the second to Conrad, should make clear the great similarity between them with regard to their symbolic preoccupations. In writing of *Moby-Dick*, Alfred Kazin has accurately observed that

> Everything in *Moby-Dick* is saturated in a mental atmosphere.
> Nothing happens for its own sake in this book, and in the midst
> of the chase, Ishmael can be seen meditating it, pulling things
> apart, drawing out its significant point.[6]

And Morton Zabel, writing of Conrad's narrative manner generally, similarly remarks that

> No attentive reader can overlook the verbal, modal, and atmos-
> pheric saturation to which he subjected his themes, or the equally
> exhaustive wringing out or draining out of them of their whole
> content of motive and consciousness.[7]

In such comments, the extremely analytic nature of Melville's and Conrad's art should be apparent. And the obsession both writers had with taking their worlds apart in the very process of "riveting" them together with realistic devices is in abundant evidence not

---

[6]"Introduction" to *Moby-Dick*, in *Melville,* ed. Chase, p. 41.
[7]"Introduction" to *The Portable Conrad* (New York, 1947), p. 34.

simply in *Moby-Dick* and "Heart of Darkness," but also in such dissecting works as "Benito Cereno," *The Confidence-Man*, and *Billy Budd*; or *The Nigger of the "Narcissus*," *Lord Jim*, *Nostromo*, and "The Secret Sharer."

If the two authors opposed the realistic trends of their day by adopting a more resonant form of expression, this was only one of the ways in which they showed their independence from a movement foreign to their more poetic sensibilities. Constantly exploring the compatibility of different narrative forms to their vision, they produced fiction elusive of all easy classification. When Ishmael is about to undertake an unprecedented physiognomical description of the whale, he proclaims: "I try all things; I achieve what I can" (*M-D*, II.1xxix.81); and his words suggest Melville's own ambitiously unregimented attitude in the book. For how many authors would attempt to assimilate in one literary work the disparate literary modes of romance, tragedy, and epic? And how many would dare borrow from, and make their own special use of, such diverse authors as Homer, Shakespeare, Milton, Carlyle, Emerson, and Hawthorne—to say nothing of the Bible itself? This willingness to experiment with different forms in the endeavor to embody ideas and themes whose intricacy defied a more conventional manner of exposition is detectable in other Melville fictions as well—most notably in *Mardi, Pierre*, "Benito Cereno," *The Confidence-Man*, and *Billy Budd.*

Unlike Melville, Conrad felt strongly that fiction should strive for a Jamesian purity and avoid using literary modes traditionally distinct from it. Nevertheless, he was equally concerned—as Ford Madox Ford has noted—with "finding a new form for the novel."[8] In the preface to *The Nigger* he inveighed against the various literary formulas (realism, romanticism, naturalism—even "sentimentalism"), and claimed that too close an attachment to any one of them ultimately blurred the writer's deepest sensitivity toward art and life (pp. xiv-xv). Going his own way, he gradually developed

[8]"Techniques," *Southern Review*, I (1935), 32.

(if he did not exactly invent) the impressionistic form of narration—a form that broke from the single, more or less omniscient, perspective and from natural chronology in order to simulate more effectively the way man most commonly encountered reality. Outside of these shifts in perspective and narrative sequence (handled most elaborately in such novels as *Lord Jim, Nostromo, Chance,* and *Victory*), Conrad's formal preoccupations generally find their parallels in Melville—as the chapter on the two writers' "nihilistic" techniques has illustrated.

If these techniques seem far more typical of the twentieth century than of the nineteenth, so do the books employing them, which compel our attention most in their concern with philosophical and moral problems directly relevant to us. Such problems, however, were not those which preoccupied the minds of either Melville's audience or Conrad's, and it is suggestive that the two authors' most profound and provocative works were ignored by their public. While Americans of the mid-nineteenth century might have responded favorably to *Typee* and *Omoo*, because these works tended to reflect their optimism about man's instinctive goodness and the world's benevolence, they turned their backs on *Moby-Dick*, a work that staunchly affirmed the immovable foundations of a morally mixed universe. And the fiction succeeding *Moby-Dick*—from *Pierre* through *The Confidence-Man*—moved steadily toward unbelief about the whole notion of ethical progression. Melville, in conscientiously giving himself up to his truer but bleaker vision, was obliged to give up his audience as well. The dark pattern of his images and symbols, his hopeless view toward his heroes, and the disastrous conclusions of his plots were all unacceptable to a public full of faith in man's ability to improve himself—and the world—by degrees. Probing the heart of man and the universe, he could find cause only for skepticism—both of man's powers to perfect himself and of nature's inherent charity and justice. Late in his life, when retreating somewhat from the despairing viewpoint that condemned his most significant fictional achievements to failure, he still continued to take exception to the popular notion that the world he inhabited was the best of all possible. Writing to a friend just six years before his death about the poet James Thomson, he remarked: "As to his pessimism, altho' neither pessimist nor optomist myself, nevertheless I relish it in the verse if for nothing else than as a counterpoise to the exorbitant hopefulness, juvenile and shallow, that makes such a bluster in these days. . . ."[9]

Conrad's formative years, which saw him accompanying his idealistic parents into their Russian exile because of his father's ardent patriotism and which also orphaned him in 1869 at the age of eleven, inclined him toward optimism no more than Melville (who at the same age had himself to witness his father's financial ruin, insanity, and death). His early life in oppressed Poland made him cynical about the ideals of progress so confidently advanced by the West, and his "twentieth-century" experiences of exile and abandonment estranged him from the mood of late nineteenth-century Victorian England. Coming, like Melville, to disbelieve in the validity (even the tenability) of all moral, religious, and philosophical doctrines, he advanced toward a position of broad skepticism. Unable to detect any moral imperative inherent either in man or the world outside him, he had to reject the entire concept of amelioration. He could see contemporary hopes only as illusory, insubstantial, and opposed to the grim facts of reality.

Such an attitude was unpalatable to a culture that optimistically, and "liberally," placed its trust in social and political reform, even in an ultimate moral reform, come the milennium. And so the English chose to ignore Conrad's greatest and most prophetic books, as the Americans earlier had ignored Melville's. These works, informed by the same weary pessimism, systematically record the futility of man's striving to make his noble ideals viable. Pierre, in his attempt to rescue the outcast Isabel, sacrifices her and himself to his quixotic ideals — and the ideals themselves are eventually recognized as meaningless. Kurtz, isolated in the wilder-

---

[9]Letter to James Billson, 22 January 1885, in *Letters*, p. 277.

ness of deepest Africa, discovers that the ethical codes he has un-questioningly followed in civilized society are completely irrelevant to his natural impulses and the primitive world surrounding him. The moral ambiguity of the two writers' most exploratory fiction at last undermines the whole concept of morality, and nothingness itself becomes an almost visible presence—as radiant as the "heart of darkness."

It is no coincidence that in recent years, as we have become increasingly conscious of our chaotic world and as the writings of the existentialists have come to permeate our thinking, interest in the two authors has soared. In many respects their vision seems more compatible with such modern novelists as Kafka, Gide, Camus, Beckett, West, and Faulkner than it does with their own contemporaries. Such modernity is explainable largely in terms of their nihilism, the mood that has pervaded most of the outstanding fiction of our day. Their disbelief in society's ability to provide the individual with reliable norms of conduct anticipates, further, the contemporary writer's preoccupation with man's perilous freedom. According to the existentialist view, man is wholly responsible for his acts; and such a responsibility is ultimately as fearsome as it is challenging, since no code of absolutes exists to sanction or censure personal decisions. In addition, as both Melville and Conrad recognized, man's condemnation to freedom defined his essential loneliness. The imperative choice of acting independently, of behaving solely with regard to "the truth of one's own sensa-tions," isolated him from his fellow-men and left him forlorn. With no set of moral prescriptions to aid him, he was obliged in deter-mining his course of behavior to rely exclusively on his own expe-rience and subjective sense of right and wrong. It is this problem of moral freedom that threatens constantly to overwhelm the modern hero, for not only has he no objective values to fall back upon, but his own psychological needs prompt him toward actions either illogical or unethical, and sometimes both. The moral uneasiness underlying much of Melville's and Conrad's fiction is easily identi-fiable with their perception of the final arbitrariness of human behavior, of "the horror" of having to act out one's accidental part in a spiritual vacuum.

The dominant literary hero of today is at battle both with himself and his surroundings. On one level, he is torn between reason and feeling, principle and passion; on another, between conventional social order and individual, often willful, anarchy. A victim of the world, he is at the same time defiant of it. An outcast of society, he is yet actively engaged with it and must eventually make his own peace with it. The alienated figures in the fiction of Melville and Conrad (from Taji, Ahab, Pierre, and Bartleby, to Kurtz, Decoud, and Heyst), by failing to find a means of reconciling themselves to the inward or outward darkness that confronts them, finally succumb to this darkness. True however in their deaths to the contradictions that have prevailed in their lives, their suicides, or near suicides, can be interpreted as signifying both their defeat and their victory. For they have at least managed to say No to the baffling, alien universe that has said No to them. The simultaneous acceptance and rejection of their fate labels them at last neither victims nor rebels, but "existential men," who ironically and equivocally combine the two categories.

The existential man is also the estranged man, and the theme of estrangement is a hallmark not only of contemporary literature but of Melville and Conrad as well. The man dangerously removed from his fellow-men is in fact their foremost subject. Even Ishmael and Marlow, often cited as providing a sane alternative to the abandonment of an Ahab or Kurtz, suffer from an isolation alleviated only in part by their willingness to share their story with others. Indeed, it may well be that one of the reasons Melville had Ishmael survive the *Pequod* disaster was that he wished to underscore his taleteller's loneliness. Rescued, Ishmael yet feels himself to be—as he resignedly puts it at the very close of the novel—"another orphan" in the universe; saved, he is left to relate his tale alone. It is surely of interest that both Ishmael and Marlow have been viewed as modern versions of the Ancient Mariner, compelled to recount their experiences in order to become reconciled to them. But inevitably, they are the heirs to their creators' skepticism about the powers of verbal communication, and their narratives are never quite able to conceal their feelings of insecurity and unrelatedness.

Still, despite their "orphan" characters, Ishmael and Marlow are meant by Melville and Conrad to be taken as spokesmen for the values of fellowship and community. The fiction of the two authors undoubtedly provides us with more salient examples of the alienated man. Probably the most "up-to-date" examples of the exile in the two writers are Bartleby and Yanko Goorall, and the pathetic fate of both, their creators seem to imply, is not exceptional but typical. When the attorney-narrator exclaims at the end of his unhappy tale: "Ah, Bartleby! Ah, humanity!" he seems to glimpse the universality of his former copyist's plight. Not simply Bartleby but everybody is essentially isolated in the prison of self and can break out of it only through illusions, whose fragility constantly subjects them to destruction. In "Amy Foster," Yanko, shipwrecked and forced to live in a foreign land among narrow-minded people temperamentally as well as culturally alien to him, suffers a fate similar to Bartleby's. The physician-narrator in this case concludes on the nature of his destiny by telling us at the very end that Yanko was a man "cast out mysteriously by the sea to perish in the supreme disaster of loneliness and despair" (*Typhoon and Other Stories*, p. 142). Beside the literal accuracy of such a statement, there is a strong indication that it is meant to portray the gloom of *every* human life. Thrust unaccountably into a world he cannot understand, man must cope with forces of hostility and indifference destined to defeat him. Though we might wish to argue that Yanko is a foreigner and therefore deficient as a "norm" for the isolated man, the fact remains that even after he has married one of the natives of the village and had a child by her, he is as far away from true assimilation as ever. And if his misfortune is to be "a wild creature under the net. . .a bird caught in a snare" (p. 141), it is also his son's—for after he has died and left his young child to be brought up according to the mores of the town, the narrator notes that the little boy, too, reminds him of "a bird caught in a snare"

(p. 142). Like his emigrant father, he will not be able to circumvent the life of futile suffering that awaits all men.

Doubtless, the pathos of this story may seem overextended in its failure to take into consideration the very real comforts of friendship and love. Even in "Bartleby," the picture of the scrivener's forlorn abandonment may appear too morbid to be representative. But however exaggerated the lonely predicaments of these pitiful figures may appear to us in our detachment, we have all at various moments understood with anguish what it is to be a Bartleby or a Yanko Goorall. Love, the traditional cure-all for man's isolation, has become less and less a solution for us as we realize, like Sartre, that loneliness is our condition on earth and that we can escape it only periodically—and then not without the introduction of a new sort of conflict. For although the absence of love may increase our alienation from the world, its onset constantly threatens to alienate us both from ourselves and reality. The dialectical treatment of love in literature today represents a clear departure from its traditional handling, and it is noteworthy that neither Melville's nor Conrad's fictional attitude toward love was typical of his age. There are no joyful marriages in Melville and not a single instance of a love relationship that culminates happily. Fayaway in *Typee* is not much more than a diversion for Tommo, Yillah is an unattainable ideal that Taji pursues at the cost of his life, and the too-alluring Isabel, by being Pierre's half sister, must become (as the hero sadly recognizes) his "bad angel." Conrad's fiction also takes a discouraged stance toward love, and in none of his important works is it offered to us as a remedy for man's existential dilemma. Yanko's marriage to Amy, far from alleviating his position in Colebrook, ends only in making his isolation more acute. But as Thomas Moser has commented in his book on Conrad:

> We must guard against being surprised, shocked or horrified at Conrad's negative attitude toward love. How could it be otherwise? Conrad sees man as lonely and morally isolated, harried by egoistic longings for power and peace, stumbling along a perilous path, his only hope benumbing labor, or, in rare cases, a

little self-knowledge. Conrad could not possibly reconcile so dark a view with a belief in the panacea of love, wife, home, and family.[10]

That the split between man and the world that has mysteriously given him life is irreparable is the fundamental tenet of absurdist thought. Much of the fiction of Melville and Conrad warrants appreciation as absurdist in its portrayal of man abandoned in a naturally hostile universe. It is a world where man, with all his ideals and aspirations, cannot but be out of place. As Stein soberly reflects in *Lord Jim*: "Sometimes it seems to me that man is come where he is not wanted, where there is no place for him. . ." (xx.208). If in both writers man attempts in vain to establish a harmonious relationship with the universe, it is because that universe must remain forever beyond his powers of knowing. And if he becomes cognizant of this estrangement, he must become tragically aware of the senselessness of his fate. Conrad once said as much himself when he remarked: "What makes mankind tragic is not that they are victims of nature, it is that they are conscious of it. . . . As soon as you know of your slavery, the pain, the anger, the strife — the tragedy begins. We can't return to nature, since we can't change our place in it."[11]

"Tragic" in this context suggests that the author's vision of man is really not so much tragic as ironic or absurd, for to be a "conscious victim" of nature is to be a figure of pathos, not tragedy. As has by now been said many times, man can be considered tragic (at least in the classic sense) only if he exists in a world governed purposefully by absolutes, a world where good and evil have objective status and are not merely "two shadows cast from one nothing." In the fiction of Melville and Conrad, man's morality is clearly of his own making and is neither supported by nor related to the universe he inhabits. Communal codes of morality, carrying no divine sanction, exist not to protect members of society from re-

---

[10]*Joseph Conrad: Achievement and Decline* (Cambridge, Mass., 1957), p. 127.

[11]31 January 1898, in *Life and Letters*, I, 226.

vengeful gods but only from themselves. Living in such a universe, the hero is desolate: confined to his subjective self, he can discover no laws having objective validity. His destiny, therefore, seems arbitrary and futile—that is, if he can formulate his difficulties at all.

This chaotic situation manifests itself artistically in the fictional form Melville and Conrad adopt to express their hero's plight. The modernity of such a form may be suggested by pointing out its relationship to the pattern of recent fiction. As Ihab Hassan has written of the contemporary American novel:

> The form reflects the inward darkness of things. . . . It acknowledges the nakedness of man by a parody of manners, quests, social or religious absolutes. . . . The form of fiction is. . .a form of ambiguities. Such ambiguities can be sustained only if the form maintains a kind of detachment. The function of form, therefore, is, first, to develop distance, and, second, to create conflicting levels of meaning, a complex interplay of points of view. Aesthetic distance in the contemporary novel is an ironic distance.[12]

Through this distance, Melville and Conrad are able simultaneously to acknowledge life's chaos and give it artistic form. Disordered, subjective reality is objectified in a pattern of calculated discrepancies. Such a literary form is well adapted for exploring the question of human values, and the fiction of the two authors is perhaps most notable in its inspection and implied criticism of conventional modes of behavior. The kind of behavior they themselves appear indirectly to recommend is generally existential: for their fiction repeatedly suggests that "the way to be" is to commit oneself to upholding those values essential both to self-realization and to the survival and moral well-being of society.

If, on the whole, the fiction of Melville and Conrad seems negative in outlook (obviously the argument of this study), all that need be said is that the nature of their truth is negative. Detecting at every turn visible evidence of the absurdity of life, they sought in

[12]*Radical Innocence: Studies in the Contemporary American Novel* (Princeton, New Jersey, 1961), pp. 116-118.

their greatest works to depict as meaningfully as possible the "proofs" of meaninglessness. Their artistic commitment to this void, again basically an existential reaction, lends affirmation to their work. For existential art, though nihilistic in its assumptions, amends nihilism by asserting man's capacity to know his absurd fate and meet it courageously. Though such art may appear restricted by the darkness at its focal point, its concerns are with nothing less than man's eternal situation. As such, the art of Melville and Conrad bears resemblance not just to contemporary fiction, but to much memorable art of the past. Their modernity is, finally, more than anything else testimony of their universality. As H. L. Mencken has written in an essay on Conrad: "[The] conviction that human life is a seeking without a finding, that its purpose is impenetrable, that joy and sorrow are alike meaningless, you will see written largely in the work of most great creative artists."[13] We may conclude, then, that the vision of Melville and Conrad is relevant not simply to the present day (as, despite audience reaction, it was relevant when it first gained artistic expression), but that it will be relevant in the future as well. For, like all outstanding artists to whom we look for insight and wisdom, Melville and Conrad are destined to be forever our contemporaries.

[13]*A Book of Prefaces* (New York, 1917), pp. 15-16.

A SELECTED BIBLIOGRAPHY

MELVILLE

Arvin, Newton. *Herman Melville.* New York: Compass Books, 1957.

Boies, J. J. "Existential Nihilism and Herman Melville," *Wisconsin Academy of Sciences, Arts, and Letters,* L (1961), 307-320.

Bowen, Merlin. *The Long Encounter: Self and Experience in the Writings of Herman Melville.* Chicago, 1960.

Carpenter, Frederic I. *American Literature and the Dream.* New York, 1955.

Chase, Richard. *The American Novel and Its Tradition.* New York: Anchor Books, c. 1957.

———, ed. *Melville: A Collection of Critical Essays.* Englewood Cliffs, N. J., 1962.

Davis, Merrell R. and William H. Gilman, eds. *The Letters of Herman Melville.* New Haven, Conn., 1960.

Feidelson, Charles. "Introduction" to *Moby-Dick.* Indianapolis, 1964.

———. *Symbolism and American Literature.* Chicago, 1953.

Fogle, Richard Harter. *Melville's Shorter Tales.* Norman, Oklahoma, 1960.

Foster, Elizabeth S. "Introduction" to *The Confidence-Man.* New York, 1954.

Gross, Seymour L., ed. *A "Benito Cereno" Handbook.* Belmont, Calif., 1965.

Howard, Leon. *Herman Melville.* Univ. of Minnesota Pamphlets on Am. Writers, No. 13. Minneapolis, 1961.

———. "Herman Melville: *Moby-Dick,*" in *The American Novel from James Fenimore Cooper to William Faulkner,* ed. Wallace Stegner. New York, 1965.

Humphreys, A. R. *Herman Melville.* New York, 1962.

Leyda, Jay. *The Melville Log: A Documentary Life of Herman Melville, 1819-1891.* 2 vols. New York, 1951.

Melville, Herman. *The Works of Herman Melville.* Standard edition. 16 vols. London: Constable & Co., 1922-24.

Miller, James E. *A Reader's Guide to Herman Melville.* New York, 1962.

Miller, Perry. "Melville and Transcendentalism," *Virginia Quarterly,* XXIX (1953), 556-575.

Murray, Henry A. "Introduction" to *Pierre.* New York, 1962.

Olson, Charles. *Call Me Ishmael.* New York, 1947.

Rhorberger, Mary. "Point of View in 'Benito Cereno': Machinations and Deceptions," *College English,* XXVII (1966), 541-546.

Sedgwick, William Ellery. *Herman Melville: The Tragedy of Mind.* Cambridge, Mass., 1944.

Seltzer, Leon F. "Camus's Absurd and the World of Melville's *Confidence-Man,"* *PMLA,* LXXXII (March 1967), 14-27.

Stafford, William T., ed. *Melville's "Billy Budd" and the Critics.* Belmont, Calif., 1961.

Stern, Milton R., ed. *Discussions of Moby-Dick.* Boston, 1960.

. *The Fine Hammered Steel of Herman Melville.* Urbana, Ill., 1957.

. "Melville's Tragic Imagination: The Hero Without a Home," in *Patterns of Commitment in American Literature,* ed. Marston LaFrance. Toronto, 1967.

Thorp, Willard. "Introduction" to *Herman Melville: Representative Selections.* New York, 1938.

CONRAD

Aubry, G. Jean. *Joseph Conrad: Life and Letters.* 2 vols. London, 1927.

Baines, Jocelyn, *Joseph Conrad: A Critical Biography.* London, 1960.

Conrad, Joseph. *Complete Works.* 26 vols. Garden City, N.Y.: Doubleday, Page & Co., 1924-26.

Curle, Richard, ed. *Conrad to a Friend: 150 Selected Letters from Joseph Conrad to Richard Curle.* London, 1928.

, *The Last Twelve Years of Joseph Conrad.* New York, 1928.

Daiches, David. *The Novel and the Modern World.* Rev. ed. Chicago, 1960.

Ford, Ford Madox. *Joseph Conrad: A Personal Remembrance.* Boston, 1924.

. "Techniques," in *Southern Review,* I (1935), 20-35.

Forster, E. M. *Abinger Harvest.* New York, 1936.

Garnett, Edward, ed. *Letters from Joseph Conrad, 1895-1924.* Indianapolis, 1928.

Gillon, Adam. *The Eternal Solitary: A Study of Joseph Conrad.* New York, 1960.

Guerard, Albert J. *Conrad the Novelist.* Cambridge, Mass., 1958.

Gurko, Leo. *Joseph Conrad: Giant in Exile.* New York, 1962.

Harkness, Bruce. *Conrad's "Heart of Darkness" and the Critics.* Belmont, Calif., 1960.

. *Conrad's "Secret Sharer" and the Critics.* Belmont, Calif., 1962.

Hewitt, Douglas. *Conrad: A Reassessment.* Cambridge, 1952.

Howe, Irving. *Politics and the Novel.* Cleveland, 1957.

Karl, Frederick R. "Conrad's Debt to Dickens," *Notes and Queries,* IV(1957), 398-400.

——. *A Reader's Guide to Joseph Conrad.* New York, 1960.

Kenner, Hugh. *Gnomon: Essays in Contemporary Literature.* New York, 1958.

Kettle, Arnold. Vol. II of *An Introduction to the English Novel.* New York: Harper Torchbooks, 1960.

Leavis, F. R. *The Great Tradition: George Eliot, Henry James, Joseph Conrad.* London, 1948.

Levine, Paul. "Joseph Conrad's Blackness," *South Atlantic Quarterly,* LXIII (1964), 198-206.

Mencken, H. L. *A Book of Prefaces.* New York, 1917.

Miller, J. Hillis. *Poets of Reality: Six Twentieth-Century Writers.* Cambridge, Mass., 1965.

Moser, Thomas. *Joseph Conrad: Achievement and Decline.* Cambridge, Mass., 1957.

Perry, John Oliver. "Action, Vision, or Voice: The Moral Dilemmas in Conrad's Tale-Telling," *Modern Fiction Studies,* X (1964), 3-14.

Stallman, R. W. *The Art of Joseph Conrad: A Critical Symposium.* East Lansing, Mich., 1960.

Tanner, Tony. "Butterflies and Beetles—Conrad's Two Truths," *Chicago Review,* XVI (1963), 123-140.

Wiley, Paul L. *Conrad's Measure of Man.* Madison, Wisconsin, 1954.

Young, Vernon. "Joseph Conrad: Outline for a Reconsideration," *Hudson Review,* II (1949), 5-19.

Zabel, Morton Dauwen. *Craft and Character in Modern Fiction.* New York, 1957.

——. "Introduction" to *Lord Jim.* Boston, 1958.

——. "Introduction" to *The Portable Conrad.* New York, 1947.

MELVILLE AND CONRAD

Canby, Henry Seidel. "Conrad and Melville," in his *Definitions: Essays in Contemporary Criticism.* New York, 1922.

Green, Jesse D. "Diabolism, Pessimism, and Democracy: Notes on Melville and Conrad," *Modern Fiction Studies,* VIII (1962), 287-305.

Guetti, James. *The Limits of Metaphor: A Study of Melville, Conrad, and Faulkner.* Ithaca, New York, 1967.

Krieger, Murray. *The Tragic Vision.* Chicago: Phoenix Books, 1966.

MacShane, Frank. "Conrad on Melville," *American Literature,* XXIX (1957-58), 463-464.

Index

Important themes and techniques in the works of Melville and Conrad are listed under each author separately. The novels and tales of the two writers are indexed independently, with subheadings where appropriate. References to their fictional characters may be found under the works in which they appear (with the exception of Marlow, who stands alone).